The **Data Toolkit**

To Dan, Jake, Grace, and Truman:
Thank you for showing me in a thousand
ways that relationships matter.

Rob

To Ray, my husband; my mom, Muriel; and my dad, David:
Thank you for your love and support, and the way in which you always modeled
putting students first in your own work in schools. You have touched the lives of many!

Pam

The **Data Toolkit**

Ten Tools for Supporting School Improvement

Robert T. Hess
Pam Robbins

Foreword by Kate Dickson

CORWIN
A SAGE Company

CORWIN
A SAGE Company

FOR INFORMATION:

Corwin
A SAGE Company
2455 Teller Road
Thousand Oaks, California 91320
(800) 233-9936
Fax: (800) 417-2466
www.corwin.com

SAGE Ltd.
1 Oliver's Yard
55 City Road
London EC1Y 1SP
United Kingdom

SAGE India Pvt. Ltd.
B 1/I 1 Mohan Cooperative Industrial Area
Mathura Road, New Delhi 110 044
India

SAGE Asia-Pacific Pte. Ltd.
33 Pekin Street #02-01
Far East Square
Singapore 048763

Acquisitions Editor: Debra Stollenwerk
Associate Editor: Desirée A. Bartlett
Editorial Assistant: Kimberly Greenberg
Project Editor: Veronica Stapleton
Copy Editor: Michelle Ponce
Typesetter: C&M Digitals (P) Ltd.
Proofreader: Dennis W. Webb
Indexer: Sheila Bodell
Cover Designer: Scott Van Atta
Permissions Editor: Adele Hutchinson

Copyright © 2012 by Corwin

Printed in the United States of America

Library of Congress Cataloging-in-Publication Data

Hess, Robert T. (Robert Thomas), 1962-

The Data toolkit : ten tools for supporting school improvement / Robert T. Hess, Pam Robbins; foreword by Kate Dickson.

p. cm.
Includes bibliographical references and index.

ISBN 978-1-4129-9297-8 (pbk.)

1. School management and organization—Data processing.
2. School management and organization—Decision making.
3. School improvement programs. I. Robbins, Pam. II. Title.

LB2806.17.H47 2012
371.2—dc23   2011040855

This book is printed on acid-free paper.

SUSTAINABLE FORESTRY INITIATIVE
Certified Chain of Custody
Promoting Sustainable Forestry
www.sfiprogram.org
SFI-01268

SFI label applies to text stock

11 12 13 14 15 10 9 8 7 6 5 4 3 2 1

Contents

Foreword

A Toolkit for Moving Forward

As we find ourselves striving to ensure that every child is prepared to pursue the challenges and opportunities of the 21st Century, we must focus on the quality of teaching and learning in every school and classroom. The authors of this book have taken a significant step as they provide a "toolkit" to help us more effectively educate *all* students in the 21st Century.

The Data Toolkit provides practical insights and practical strategies to facilitate effective teaching and learning. It supports educators in analyzing data in a way that will empower higher-quality decision making related to curriculum, instruction, and assessment. Ultimately, if implemented well, this process will result in high student achievement and greater staff collaboration.

Most important, this book is not a typical set of formulas designed to aggregate, disaggregate, and manipulate data to identify highly successful schools or schools that are struggling. In contrast, it elegantly reflects Margaret Wheatley's theory of high-performing systems. It is the complex and continuous interaction between vision and purpose, data and information, and relationships that creates the synergy to generate high-performing systems. As Wheatley so thoughtfully suggests: ultimately, it is all about relationships.

This unique resource provides a fresh and holistic view of what it takes to support all educational stakeholders in creating high-performing schools and school communities. It places adults and children in context as a community that must work cooperatively to ensure the success of all. The blending of the high-touch and high-tech approaches is exactly what we need to achieve success for all schools and children.

This book is a major contribution to the field of education as it defines the essential work that education stakeholders need to engage in to realize our goals of educating *all* students in a world full of future possibilities and challenges. I trust that school board members, superintendents, principals, teachers, and parents will use it as they come together to create great schools.

As Albert Einstein so candidly said, "The significant problems we have cannot be solved at the same level of thinking at which we created them."

This toolkit provides breakthrough ideas, direction, and possibilities for moving all of our schools forward.

Kate Dickson, PhD

President, Leadership Matters, Inc.

Chalkboard Project Advisor

Preface

We have entered an age of accountability with increased demands for performance and decreased resources. There are concerns about preparing students with the right knowledge and skills for the 21st-century workplace and equipping them with the critical-thinking skills to face challenges that have yet to be defined. Together, these conditions place unprecedented pressure on schools to do more with less. The need to analyze student performance data, scrutinize which practices produce promising results, and identify interventions that must be implemented when desirable results are absent has never been greater. Together, these demands inspired the development of *The Data Toolkit*.

The Data Toolkit was designed with two purposes in mind:

- To provide classroom teachers and other school leaders, schools, and districts with practical quantitative and qualitative instruments to analyze data in a meaningful way and contribute to changes in practice that ultimately enhance staff and student learning
- To highlight a wide array of specific tools that can be used to examine a variety of data. Embedded in the use of each of these tools is a process that both builds community and focuses on results

The emphasis of each tool is not just on examining, charting, or graphing data but rather propelling individuals and teams to action with a plan informed by data and focused on results.

WHY THIS BOOK? ■

Most schools are swamped with data, and staff members often feel overwhelmed and immobilized by them. Many times they are unable to find meaning and derive next steps from their data. Douglas B. Reeves (2010), in a "Leadership and Learning Blog" referred to these conditions with the phrase "Drowning in Data; Thirsty for Information." Even when educators know a problem exists, they often don't have a process that delineates what to do next. This may result in a lack of improvement or action, but it is not for lack of caring or trying.

Data paralysis, as opposed to data analysis, often occurs because teams do not have a structure to help them reflect upon data and ask meaningful questions about the data in order to clarify and identify the problem that needs to be solved. Once the problem is understood fully, then action planning can occur. Teachers, administrators, and support staff need specific tools to generate meaningful data, illuminate relationships between instructional interventions and student performance data, and facilitate conversations so that appropriate and responsive interventions can be designed, implemented, and carefully monitored, with the end result being high levels of student learning. In the process, teachers and administrators learn as well. Hence, the capacity to produce the desired results over time is created. That is where the data tools come in. Data tools help frame the questions, drive the conversation, and lead to reflection—the most vital part of the data team process. Reflection is generated by the questions posed and pondered. Once understanding is uncovered, a data-driven plan with a focus on desired results can be crafted.

The Data Toolkit provides easy-to-use tools that support educators in understanding and analyzing what they have accomplished in classrooms and to determine what to do next. These tools help staff members move beyond just talking about their data to taking learning-focused decisive actions that make a difference in the lives of their students, the skillfulness of staff, and the health of their schools.

The book's chapters focus on

1. Providing a broad spectrum of meaningful tools to analyze data with the goal of directing action for school improvement efforts

2. Identifying specific processes to be used with each instrument/tool, which galvanize the collective expertise of staff members on data teams and will engage individuals in building norms for collaboration, respect for diverse perspectives, and trust in the process

3. Presenting examples of how data teams, professional learning communities (PLCs), and individual teachers in schools have actually used the tools in their own settings

4. Highlighting stories and examples of successful school improvement and reform efforts occurring around the country in which the analysis and meaningful use of data played a central role

■ USING THE DATA TOOLKIT

The tools are organized in a progressive manner from setting the stage (tools to help teams get started looking at data), quantitative tools (for analyzing numerical data), and qualitative tools (for analyzing questions, problems, and taking action). Teams or individuals can use the tools. They can be used by an entire staff and in individual classrooms by teachers as they examine student performance. Their use is limited only by one's imagination!

There are two types of data: quantitative and qualitative. Quantitative data are primarily expressed in numbers. Qualitative data are primarily expressed in words. Quantitative data can be easily measured and compared. Grade point averages (GPAs), student absences, and the percentage of students who pass a test are all quantitative data. Quantitative data are most often expressed via spreadsheets, charts, and graphs.

Qualitative data, on the other hand, are best expressed through story and are collected through observations, conversations, interviews, and surveys. For example, it is only through qualitative data that we understand *why* a student is missing 30 days of school. Even though quantitative data are most easily produced and distributed, qualitative data are absolutely essential to helping schools and districts improve. If all our plans and strategies are based on numbers alone, our implementation efforts will miss the mark, and we will end up with unintended consequences, plans that don't make sense, and activities that do not reach the intended outcome. Both quantitative and qualitative data sources are vital to every school and district improvement effort. Quantitative data (numbers) help us to see. They prevent positive illusions. Qualitative data (stories) help us to understand. They prevent unintended consequences.

School improvement hinges on being able to use both quantitative and qualitative approaches to data. Both types of tools are used throughout this book, and when faced with complex problems, practitioners often use a combination of tools and approaches to see results. The bottom line when it comes to all improvement efforts is the ability to do something differently by leveraging data in such a way that a team's actions are effective in terms of outcomes and efficient in terms of resources.

Setting the Stage

The first three tools, Build Your Team, Identify the Problem, and Three Guiding Questions, set the stage for deep data analysis by helping educators build a sound foundation to effectively analyze data. As mentioned earlier, data analysis can be conducted by individuals or teams. Effective teams understand their members and develop norms to govern their behavior. These teams also realize that data alone don't solve problems. It is only as a result of asking questions about data that individuals can discover what needs to be done and how to orchestrate and implement effective interventions.

Quantitative Tools

The next three tools, Analyze Your Students, Four Quadrants, and Wagon Wheel are all tools that address and work with numbers. Analyzing Your Students attaches one set of numbers to each student. Four Quadrants attaches two sets of numbers to each student, and the Wagon Wheel can attach multiple sets of numbers to students, grade levels, or schools. Using tools that deal with numbers is a great starting place for many teams because plotting data according to a tool removes all judgment from the initial conversation and helps teams move from understanding the data to developing plans to address the data and create desired results.

Qualitative Tools

In the next portion of the book, three qualitative tools are introduced: Five Whys, Relations Diagram, and Fishbone. These are predominantly tools that engage teams in problem solving through discussion, speculation, and interaction. These qualitative tools help teams understand the story behind the numbers.

The Five Whys tool is used to help teams explore the root causes of a problem. The Relations Diagram helps teams identify which problem's cause drives other causes, so that interventions can be effectively constructed. The Fishbone combines elements of the previous qualitative and quantitative tools and provides data teams with a structured framework for exploring the reasons behind a success (improved test scores, for instance) or a cause for concern (poor attendance). The Fishbone presented in this book provides a reflection component, ranking of reasons, and strategies for taking an improvement to the next level.

School Improvement Mapping

The final tool, School Improvement Mapping (SIM), fosters synergy as a result of multiple data sources. Through this tool, a team can design an action plan that will make a difference in student learning and achievement outcomes. It includes a process for designating specific steps for implementation of an action plan. The SIM helps faculty members begin with the end in mind and accomplish that end based on an action plan informed by performance data.

Special Features

Each chapter of *The Data Toolkit* begins with a meaningful quote and vignette designed to illustrate the application of the featured tool, followed by a description of how the tool is used in the school setting and a real world example of practitioners using the tool. Throughout each chapter there are additional stories of how the tool can be used by teachers and other school leaders. Educational reform and improvement efforts are highlighted throughout the book as they relate to the tools being presented. In addition, each chapter concludes with an "In the Field" and "Putting It all Together" feature that showcases how a school team has used that particular tool to support their school improvement efforts.

The book concludes with a chapter titled "Now What?" There, the reader will find blackline masters of each tool, along with several suggestions for potential classroom, team, school, and district uses of the tools. *The Data Toolkit* is designed to provide practitioners with everything they need to apply each tool in a variety of settings. As authors, we wish you the best in making meaning from your data and using it in ways that lead to staff and student learning and achievement!

Acknowledgments

Corwin would like to thank the following individuals for taking the time to provide their editorial insight:

Florie Buono, Assistant Principal for Curriculum & Instruction
Gulf High School
New Port Richey, FL

Carrie Carpenter, Instructional Coach
Redmond School District 2J
Redmond, OR

Scott Hollinger, Instructional Coach for Principals and Teachers
Communities Foundation of Texas: Texas High School Project
McAllen, TX

Virginia E. Kelsen, Assistant Principal
Rancho Cucamonga High School
Rancho Cucamonga, CA

Patricia Jo McDivitt, Senior VP, Curriculum, Instruction, and Assessment
Data Recognition Corporation
Plymouth, MN

Charre Todd, Science Teacher
Crossett Middle School
Crossett, AR

About the Authors

Robert T. Hess is a practicing superintendent with 10 years of experience as a secondary teacher. He has been an administrator at the high school, middle school, and K through 8 levels and served in the central office as a student achievement leader, and assistant superintendent. He is currently the superintendent of the Lebanon Community School District located in Lebanon, Oregon. In 2003, he founded Breakthrough Schools, a grassroots network of educators dedicated to helping schools and districts achieve breakthrough school improvement results. He earned his doctorate from the University of Oregon and has taught classes at the University of Oregon, Oregon State University, Willamette University, and Lewis & Clark College on the following subjects: teacher leadership, professional development for administrators, priority leadership, school improvement planning, data analysis for school improvement, and research for education.

The Data Toolkit is his fourth book. He frequently presents on the topics of teacher leadership, professional learning communities, school culture, quality school improvement, and teacher/principal evaluation systems. His webpage can be visited at *www.thedatacoach.net*, and he can be reached by e-mail at robhess1@mac.com.

Pam Robbins earned her doctorate in educational administration from the University of California, Berkeley. Currently, she consults with school systems, professional organizations, state departments of education, leadership academies, and corporations throughout the United States, Canada, Great Britain, Europe, Asia, and South America. Her presentation topics include professional learning communities, effective teaching, how the brain learns, emotional intelligence, leadership, teaching in the block schedule, peer coaching, school culture, and presentation skills. Pam has served as a teacher, high school basketball coach, administrator, director of special projects and research, and director of training for the North Bay California Leadership Academy. She has lectured at several universities, authored and coauthored books, and developed training materials for several principals' academies. She may be contacted by e-mail at probbins@shentel.net.

Introduction

Continuous improvement in schools is predicated upon analyzing and responding to data. Staff and student learning is the goal of continuous improvement. School improvement plans and the work of professional learning communities (PLCs) both focus on the identification of data needed to assess results, data collection, analysis, and action planning. Research on PLCs substantiates the claim that in schools where professional colleagues work together to study, analyze, and respond to data, learning soars.

USING THIS BOOK ■

This book may be used in a variety of ways. For example, it may be used for a professional "book talk." In this context, all staff members read the book and reflect together about its content. Staff members may select a favorite tool they read about and share it along with their vision for how it may be used. Questions could be developed such as "What tool(s) would be best to use to determine how to increase the use of higher order thinking skills?" Staff members could then participate in a scavenger hunt through the book to identify the most appropriate tools. In a faculty, team, or department meeting, faculty members can examine one or two tools per meeting and practice using them with site-level data.

The chapters are written so that they may be read in any order with the broad goal of increasing the repertoire of practical tools that data teams possess to examine and analyze data. Each chapter includes

- a description of a data analysis tool,
- an explanation of the conditions under which this particular tool might be used,
- the steps to using the tool,
- a graphic depicting what the tool looks like when it is used,
- stories about how school staff members have used the tool,
- education theory and philosophy that supports the use of the tool, and
- reflections/insights on using the tool.

THE DATA TOOLS ■

These tools were developed over the last several years by working collaboratively with principals and teachers with their data in school settings. Educators were constantly looking for ways to make meaning from their data, and found these particular tools extremely helpful. These tools actually increased educators' data fluency, a term used to describe what happens when people actually begin to use the mass of data that surrounds them in such a way that instruction is adjusted and improved. Some of these tools have their foundation in Edward Deming's (1986) work around quality and continuous improvement, which has been impacting practices in the industry for over 50 years. These tools have been simplified and tailored for use in educational settings. Some of these tools are new to the field, based on the work of the authors, and others have been adapted from university settings, research studies, work within data teams, and teachers looking to use and learn from data in their classrooms. All of the tools embody best practices regarding the use of data. This book and these tools facilitate thinking and conversation about using data so that teams of administrators and teachers can collaborate in solving problems and generate school improvement at the classroom, school, and district level.

■ CHAPTER OVERVIEW

In the paragraphs that follow, the focus of each chapter's content is summarized as a quick reference for the reader.

Chapter 1: Build Your Team

Effective work with data is done in teams. Forming a team is a critical component of the work. This chapter addresses what you need to think about in forming data teams and what structures are necessary to ensure that a team is functioning well. Great teams need dedicated time to work and structures that ensure everyone is involved, engaged, and take responsibility for the work.

Chapter 2: Identify the Problem

Understanding your data and knowing what data tool to use begins by being able to define the problem you are seeking to solve. This chapter emphasizes the importance of reflection when approaching a problem and provides helpful reflection tools for getting started. The process of reflection helps staff members to address tough issues through conversations and realize that success often comes as a result of analyzing failure.

Chapter 3: The Three Guiding Questions

Collecting data begins with defining what you are going to teach and how you will know that your students have learned the knowledge and skills you have identified as outcomes. Many staff members look beyond this critical step in the process by looking immediately at summative data before they understand and agree on the learning targets. Unpacking standards to identify learning targets is step number one followed closely by determining what assessments you will use to measure progress toward those learning targets. Using this tool on a regular basis will help staff members understand and own the data they are gathering.

Chapter 4: Analyze Your Students

Data that drive change must drill down to the individual-student level. It is only when we analyze our data through a lens that focuses upon the individual student that we can begin planning for action with the specificity required to produce results. This chapter presents a simple tool and framework to put students into blue, green, yellow, and red zones based upon a given data set. For example, if the instruction (prevention and intervention strategies) is effective, 80% of the students will be in the green (meeting) and blue (exceeding) zones. These students do not need additional instruction or support. Another 10% to 15% of the students are in the yellow zone, which means they need an additional dose of instruction at their rate and level to be successful.

We know from research and experience that the best solution for increasing learning is tailored instruction and additional time. Students most at risk (5%) require another dose of instruction tailored to their needs. Helping teachers see their students in terms of need by placing them into these four categories is the purpose of the Analyze Your Students tool. After doing this activity, there is profound clarity about what each student needs and ideas emerge through collaboration about how to meet those needs.

Chapter 5: Four Quadrants

The Four Quadrants tool enables teams of teachers to compare two sets of data and graph that data into quadrants so that decisions can be made regarding which intervention to use and when to use it. Teachers choose sets of data that are related to one another such as reading fluency and reading comprehension so that they can see the relationship these data points have to each other. For instance, a student who understands what he reads but reads slowly (lack of fluency) needs a different intervention than a student who is fluent but doesn't understand what she is reading. This tool is powerful for providing clear direction regarding what intervention a student needs in order to reach his or her full potential as a learner.

Chapter 6: Wagon Wheel

The last of the quantitative tools, the Wagon Wheel enables educators to compare and contrast multiple data sets by placing corresponding data points along the spokes of a wheel. For example, if one is comparing writing scores across schools or the reading scores of different subgroups, this compare and contrast tool exposes patterns that can lead to strategic actions that generate improvement and help teams achieve intended results as opposed to unintended consequences. Whereas the previous tools are best suited for individual classrooms or grade levels, this quantitative tool is best used to analyze data at the school or district level.

Chapter 7: Five Whys

Developed by Toyota engineers who were trained to ask five *why* questions for every problem they encountered, this tool helps educators see and understand that every problem is connected to other problems and that solving complex problems only occurs when we get to the root cause of the problem and address it. The Five Whys is a systems-thinking tool that helps teachers and administrators think outside the box for solutions and identify actions that have a powerful impact on results. This qualitative tool helps educators explore the relationship between causes and helps identify strategies to address complex and persistent problems.

Chapter 8: Relations Diagram

When staff members or teams are faced with entrenched, complex, persistent problems, the Relations Diagram can be used to determine the key drivers of a particular problem so that interventions can be targeted, strategic, and effective. This tool begins by having staff members identify and agree on the problem to be solved. Once agreement is reached, all of the possible causes are brainstormed and presented in a circle around the problem. From there, each cause is individually analyzed to determine its impact on other causes as well as the problem. Through the Relations Diagram, a team can address a problem and get to the root cause of that problem so that an effective strategy can be developed. Through this process, the team discovers one or more causes that influence many others. Once the driving causes are determined, team members can propose, agree on, and eventually implement strategies that lead to effective solutions. A Relations Diagram process greatly increases stakeholder commitment and ownership to solve persistent problems together.

Chapter 9: The Fishbone

The Fishbone tool has been used in business settings for some time to analyze cause and effect data. With this tool, teachers can choose an outstanding result or cause for concern and examine specific reasons that led to those results. By taking the time to reflect and rate the effectiveness of each reason, staff members can identify key drivers in their data that led to an outstanding result or eliminate factors that detract from their success. In many ways, the Fishbone tool combines the quantitative and qualitative elements of the previous six tools because it takes into account both numbers and causes to determine a solid course of action.

Chapter 10: School Improvement Mapping

Similar to the Five Whys, School Improvement Mapping (SIM) helps data teams chart their improvement efforts and keep track of what they are doing strategically to take action. This tool is best used in conjunction with other tools because it helps crystallize team efforts so that interventions and actions will have a lasting impact. SIM adds a measure of accountability to the work of data teams.

We invite you to begin your learning journey, exploring the tools and stories that have been tucked into the pages that follow. May your journey be productive and may it add to your collective knowledge base to enhance teaching and learning for all students.

1

Build Your Team

The man who goes alone can start today; but he who travels with another must wait till that other is ready, and it may be a long time before they get off.

—Henry David Thoreau

The quote above illustrates one of the most challenging elements of data team work—getting started. Research confirms that in schools where professional learning communities (PLCs) exist, those schools are four times more likely to be improving academically than in those schools where faculty members operate in isolation (Ann Lewis in Schmoker, 2011). Many times, faculty members have been to trainings and read books, but for some reason—perhaps many reasons—fall short in the actual implementation of effective PLCs that gather, analyze, and use data in meaningful ways to improve outcomes for students and working conditions for adults. If a team waits until all members are ready, meaningful work may not get done. Sometimes, team members just have to decide to get started. Using the 10 data tools in this book helps a team get ready and embark upon the journey of improvement. A successful journey is dependent upon positive relationships and trust among professional colleagues. Positive relationships begin with understanding one's teammates.

THE POWER OF RELATIONSHIPS ■

The quality of relationships among professional colleagues in an organization has a profound impact on the organization's productivity, its workplace climate, and the quality of its outcomes. Collaboration creates talent, diverse perspectives, and synergy. Conflict among professional colleagues destroys these—sending individuals packing. The data analysis tools in the following chapters can be used by individuals but yield the richest outcomes if they are used by collaborating members of learning communities, such as data teams.

Often the pressure of deadlines for reports, rigorous timelines, and strategic plans causes organizational members to rush to begin doing the work, such as analyzing data, rather than taking time to reflect upon the nature of the work to be done and how they might prepare to do the work. As a consequence, schools often find themselves *data rich* and *information poor*. If data teams have not taken time to talk about how they do the work and developed norms to govern themselves, many find themselves in conflict internally. As a result, time and effort are diverted from the task of analyzing data. When this happens, data team members find excuses to skip meetings and team effort disintegrates. This chapter is strategically placed before the others because there is a critical need to address how to do the work before the work of data analysis actually begins.

Recently, a high school math teacher who had been on a data team reflected,

> As a result of talking about how we want to be treated as team members, what our beliefs about teaching and learning were, and how we would want to address conflict before we got into analyzing site-level data, I learned much about some of my colleagues with whom I had shared coffee for ten years but never really knew!

How a workplace feels—the emotional climate—impacts both morale and productivity. In the paragraphs that follow, we offer strategies to enhance the quality of working relationships among members of data teams as they embark upon using the data analysis tools in their own settings. These strategies also contribute to building a more collaborative, learning-focused workplace, a key ingredient in highly successful schools.

■ TOOL 1: THE SMALLEY TEAM-BUILDING PERSONALITY TEST

The personality test developed by Dr. Gary Smalley and Dr. John Trent is a tool teams have found helpful (Smalley & Trent, 1999). This brief assessment (see Tool 1 on page 123 for a blank version to photocopy) can be completed in just a few minutes and correlates to the more extensive Dominance, Influence, Steadiness, Compliance (DISC) personality tests that were developed in 1928 by John Geier and the work of Dr. William Marston (Moulton, 1999). Smalley and Trent have linked the four components of DISC to the character traits of four animals: lion (dominance), otter (influence), golden retriever (steadiness), and beaver (compliance).

Each column in Figure 1.1 represents an animal based on its personality traits and the relational and communicative strengths and weakness of each personality trait for team settings. Most people tend to have one or two dominate personality types. One of the keys to developing high-functioning teams is to understand the traits of each team member and how he or she contributes to working together effectively for the common good of all students.

Figure 1.1 Interpreting the Results

	The Lion	The Otter	The Golden Retriever	The Beaver
Team member strengths	Takes charge, is a problem solver, competitive, confrontational, and enjoys change.	Optimistic, energetic, motivates others, and is future oriented.	Warm and relational, loyal, enjoys routine, is a peacemaker, sensitive, and feeling.	Accurate, precise, focuses on quality control, discerning, and analytical.
Team member weaknesses	Direct or impatient, busy, cold-blooded, impulsive or takes big risks, and insensitive to others.	Unrealistic or daydreamer, impatient, manipulator or pushy, and avoids details or lacks follow-through.	Misses opportunities, stays in a rut, sacrifices own feelings for harmony, and is easily hurt or holds a grudge.	Critical or strict, too controlling, pessimistic of new opportunities, and loses overview.
Preferred communication style	Direct or blunt, one-way communicator, and weakness—not a good listener.	Can inspire others, optimistic or enthusiastic, one-way communicator, and weakness—high energy can be used to manipulate others.	Indirect, two-way communicator, great listener, and weakness—uses too many words or provides too many details.	Factual, two-way communicator. great listener, and weakness—desire for detail and precision can frustrate others.
Team structure needs	Recognition, responsibility, opportunity to solve problems, and challenging activities.	Approval, opportunity to verbalize, visibility, and social recognition.	Emotional security and agreeable environment.	Quality and exact expectations.
Actions to improve	Add softness and become a great listener.	Be attentive to others and be more optimistic.	Learn to say *no* and to confront.	Understand that total support is not always possible.

Source: Smalley and Trent, 1999. Available at http://smalley.cc/marriage-assessments/free-personality-test

In the Smalley model, team members discover the major and minor personality traits that correspond to accompanying strengths and weaknesses. When team members understand one another, their ability to work together and form a strong bond is enhanced. As a result, the team is more productive and effective.

Lion

- Strengths: visionary, practical, productive, independent, decisive, leader
- Weaknesses: cold, domineering, self-sufficient, unforgiving, sarcastic

Otter

- Strengths: outgoing, warm, friendly, talkative, enthusiastic, compassionate
- Weaknesses: undisciplined, unproductive, exaggerates, egocentric, unstable

Golden retriever

- Strengths: calm, easygoing, dependable, quiet, objective, diplomatic
- Weaknesses: selfish, stingy, procrastinator, unmotivated, indecisive, fearful

Beaver

- Strengths: analytical, self-disciplined, industrious, organized, sacrificing
- Weaknesses: moody, self-centered, touchy, negative, unsociable, critical

Another Team-Building Strategy: Using Objects to Reflect Personalities

Individuals are polite when they first begin working together. But as time goes on, personality differences and differences in beliefs about teaching and learning tend to surface as the team examines data. These differences can gradually lead to conflict, diverting focus from the task of data analysis and action planning. To reduce the possibility of this happening, it is useful to take time to do a personality inventory (Figure 1.2). While many inventories exist from which to choose, Harvey Silver, speaking to a group of participants at an Association for Supervision and Curriculum Development (ASCD) conference in New Orleans, once shared a "four-paneled windowpane" of personalities featuring household objects and asked participants, "Are you more like a paper clip, magnifying glass, teddy bear, or slinky?" He then asked participants to brainstorm attributes of each object and record the information in the window-pane labeled with that object.

After the information was recorded, participants were asked to analyze their perceptions of which object was most like their personality, noting "the intent is not to put anyone in a box," but rather to reflect upon personality attributes and traits. Participants then went to one of the four corners of the room, each labeled with one of the household objects, to indicate their perceptions of their own personality styles. Doing this activity helped faculty members in one school better understand actions and reactions of their colleagues during their work as a data team.

During this activity one teacher reflected,

I always thought Justin was *unfeeling* as a person. As a result of doing the personality windowpanes, I realized he was a paperclip and really

Figure 1.2 Personality Inventory

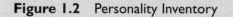

Paper Clip	Magnifying Glass
• Organized	• Asks questions
• Punctual	• Detailed
• Neat	• Thinker
• Practical	• Observant
Teddy Bear	**Slinky**
• Relational	• Humorous
• Warm	• Energetic
• People first	• Visionary
• Friendly	• Talkative

was *task first, relationship second* in his work style. I, on the other hand, was a teddy bear who valued *relationships first and tasks second*. I came to understand why Justin perceived me as *fluffy*. And sometimes, he hurt my feelings. It also helped us realize why Carmella always asked *why* questions. It turned out that she was a magnifying glass and really wasn't asking questions to stall us in decision making but honestly needed to know *why* before she could move forward. Understanding the impact of personality styles on our working relationships gave us a tool to express discomfort, dissatisfaction, or frustration in our work. It helped us separate practice from person. It enabled us to enhance the quality of the work we did as a team because we could identify how specific behaviors were impacting processes, such as brainstorming, in which we were engaged.

HIGH-FUNCTIONING TEAMS ■

Teamwork is difficult and complex. High-performance teams understand differences in style and personality and learn how to manage or prevent disappointment in performance or unnecessary conflicts. Many times, individuals on teams become irritated because other members of the team come late to meetings, text during meetings, or don't fulfill their commitment to the team. To address these maladies, successful teams take the time to develop norms to govern working relationships. There are a number of approaches to developing norms. One is to give each member of the data team two sticky notes and ask them to write how they wish to be treated during meetings on one sticky note. On the other, write how they wish the team to function. When they have finished this individual task, ask them to share what they have written. Suggest that they build categories of sticky notes based on similarity of content.

For instance, what would the category be if four sticky notes read the following?

- I wish to be treated with respect.
- Respect.
- Listen to one another and treat each other with respect.
- Honor and respect each member's contributions.

The category name, based on similarity of content, would be *respect*. After categories are formed and named, group members create norms to assure that each category is addressed. For example, the category labeled *respect* might be addressed with a norm that reads, "We agree to treat all team members and their contributions with respect."

The norms are then posted and group members are asked if any changes are needed or if they support governing themselves with the norms as written. If members support the norms, they sign the norm document. Each member of the team receives a signed copy of the document. A large print version of this is posted where the team meets. Norms are reviewed before the work of data analysis is begun, revisited during the meeting if members are not adhering to the norms to which they agreed, and reflected upon at the end of every work session. During the initial few meetings, this action may seem artificial and awkward, but over time it provides an avenue for addressing unproductive behaviors and increasing productivity.

In an effort to improve performance, a data team brainstormed actions that "pushed their buttons" or irritated them, then planned proactively what they would do if that action occurred. The list included things, such as

- coming to a meeting late,
- side conversations,
- texting or doing other work during the meeting,
- dominating a discussion in a way that precludes others' participation,
- putting others down, and
- not following through with commitments.

By creating this list ahead of time, not only were team members able to brainstorm consequences but the list also provided a way to make public the expectations for interactions within the data team meetings.

Improvement Means Change, and Change Means Conflict

Although there are strategies teams can use to prevent unnecessary conflict, not being afraid of conflict and dealing with it appropriately when it occurs are trademarks of data teams that are committed to improving outcomes through effective change. In the best-selling leadership fable, *The Five Dysfunctions of a Team* (Lencioni, 2002), Patrick Lencioni addresses the five pitfalls of teams:

- absence of trust,
- fear of conflict,
- lack of commitment,
- avoidance of accountability, and
- inattention to results.

Although any one of these areas could be problematic, school data teams most frequently struggle with a fear of conflict. Staffed with adults who work with children for their avocation, one can understand why the fear of conflict and avoiding conflict at all costs is so prevalent in schools. Most teachers are not accustomed to or trained to work with adults. Teacher preparation programs focus on developing the teaching skills of the individual teacher. There is very little team or case-based learning. Even though we know the most effective learning happens in groups, schools have for generations been organized as collections of individual adults who work with groups of children. Being able to work through conflict in order to initiate change that leads to improvement is something every effective data team must be able to do on a regular basis.

The first step in overcoming conflict is getting past the idea that conflict is negative. Conflict is a reality for teams that do meaningful work together and try to improve outcomes. Improvement does not occur without doing something differently. Doing things differently requires change, and change is uncomfortable for most people. In his recent book, *Leading Change in Your School*, Douglas Reeves (2009) identifies seven myths that get in the way of change and school improvement efforts:

- Myth 1, plan your way to greatness—Research shows that large, complex strategic plans are actually *inversely* related to growth in student achievement gains. If a plan must be written, keep it to a page and start with a clear vision and values.
- Myth 2, just a little bit better is good enough—Deep implementation takes time and commitment. Breakthrough results do not happen quickly.
- Myth 3, we want you to change us . . . really—Any change meets with resistance because change is loss. People who demand change generally direct that change at others, not themselves.
- Myth 4, people love to collaborate—In the early stages, collaboration is not something people seek or enjoy, but only those committed to collaboration are able to effectively implement data teams in their schools.
- Myth 5, hierarchy changes systems—It is relationships within the network (the people actually doing the work) that bring about sustainable change, not authority. Hierarchy is limited by time and resources. Networks and teams of individuals are not.
- Myth 6, volume equals VOLUME—The loudest voices do not represent the majority. There is never 100% agreement for any change. When

leaders invest their time and energy into those who want to improve, breakthroughs become reality.

- Myth 7, the leader is the perfect composite of every trait—Hero leadership does not get the job done. It takes a team.

In order to overcome these myths, teams must embrace and work through conflict to experience success. Schools and organizations that seek to avoid conflict by burying it or pretending it doesn't exist eventually stall in the implementation of their improvement efforts. Ideas on how to improve are a dime a dozen—very cheap and easy to come by. Being able to actually *implement* change that endures and results in lasting improvement is difficult and does not occur without high-functioning teams willing and able to work through the myths and conflicts associated with change.

Understanding How Change Occurs

In the best-selling book, *Switch: How to Change When Change Is Hard*, Heath and Heath (2010) discuss the role of understanding, emotions, and boundaries (or pathways) when it comes to implementing effective change. Some change efforts simply require someone to understand why the change is necessary. For instance, smoking in America dramatically decreased when the Surgeon General stamped the ill effects of using tobacco on the label (understanding). However, some people today continue to smoke even though they know it is bad for them because they are emotionally attached to the habit. Quitting for those folks requires intensive support or the establishment of boundaries (real or imaginary) that prevent them from accessing cigarettes. Every improvement activity requires some sort of shift or change. Effective leaders help staff members to understand that friction or conflict is a necessary part of the equation and they work with people's emotions around change to help people make the switch. They also create structures or boundaries to support meaningful change.

■ TEAM MEMBER ROLES AND RESPONSIBILITIES

Another useful strategy for working with data teams is to have rotating role responsibilities. For example, the roles and responsibilities described in Figure 1.3 might be assigned to individual members.

The role assignments usually last just one meeting and then the individual who has played a specific role nominates another team member to assume that role for the next meeting. Rotating role responsibilities assures that team members stay engaged and learn how to support and understand one another in the various components of the work.

TIPS Framework for Data Teams

Developed by Dr. Rob Horner and Dr. Anne Todd (2010) at the University of Oregon, the TIPS data team framework stands for Team Initiated Problem Solving. Using this model (illustrated in Figure 1.4) clearly communicates what

Figure 1.3 Team Member Roles and Responsibilities

Role	Responsibility
Facilitator	Call meeting to order, outline work to be done, clarify communications, remind team members of norms if they are not being followed, and summarize proceedings at the end of the meeting.
Recorder	Record contributions of individual members on chart paper or electronically.
Observer / encourager	Observe verbal contributions and body language and encourage quiet members of the group to add their perspectives to the dialogue and the work.
Climate / norms monitor	Monitors climate of the work group, calls group members' attention to moments of discomfort, and suggests solution strategies.
Timekeeper	Reminds group members of how much time has elapsed and how much remains for a given task.

Figure 1.4 TIPS Framework for Data Teams

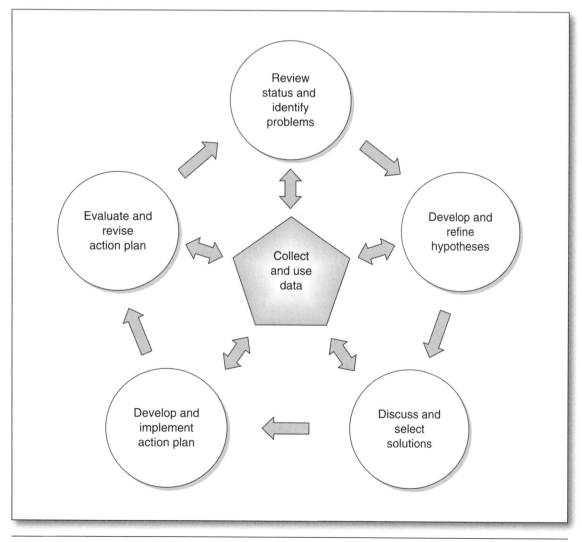

Source: Horner and Todd, 2010

is expected at each stage. In this model, data teams conduct the following five activities during each meeting:

- review status and identify problems,
- develop and refine hypothesis,
- discuss and select solutions,
- develop and implement action plan, and
- evaluate and revise action plan.

In the TIPS model, the data team has four distinct roles that members play: facilitator, minute taker, data analyst, and active team member. It is the facilitator's responsibility to chair the meeting, move the team members through the five stages in a timely manner, and make sure everyone is participating and actively involved. Although everyone is responsible to think about the data presented and use it to make decisions, it is the data analyst's job to make sure the right data are brought to the meeting and describe to the team what the data represent so that they can be used effectively to make decisions.

The minute taker is responsible for tracking the problems the team identifies, the proposed solutions, and team member's actions. This is done electronically as the meeting progresses and sent to team members at the end of the meeting. The rest of the team members are active participants who come to the meeting prepared to participate in a meaningful way, think, and take action as necessary. TIPS is designed so that efficiency and effectiveness are the cornerstones of data meetings that lead to team members taking action and keeping each other accountable for results.

■ ADDITIONAL HELPFUL HINTS

Staff members are busy professionals. While no time is ideal for a data team meeting, scheduling the meeting in advance, along with identifying the desired outcomes at the end of the previous meeting, allows members of the team to plan proactively. Publishing an agenda ahead of time with time allocations for each agenda item also contributes to team productivity.

If team members need to come to a meeting having studied data, provide them with that data at least a week in advance. If homework is to be assigned, ask two people to be responsible. This eases the burden of work and encourages collaboration. If team members are unfamiliar with knowledge of how to disaggregate data by group, such as low socioeconomic status (SES), conduct training as needed. This provides critical foundational skills for the work that data teams do.

Analyzing data and action planning based on that data is difficult work. Taking time to acknowledge and celebrate the contributions of team members and the accomplishments of the team can boost morale and create energy for future collaborative work. Providing feedback on the results of implementing action plans developed from data analysis can create a sense of efficacy and momentum for continuing to do the work that culminates in student learning gains.

The chapters that follow provide a wide array of data analysis tools applicable to a spectrum of unique contexts. Together with the process skills from this chapter, the content regarding data tools, illustrated with specific examples, add to the reader's repertoire of strategies to enhance the quality of teaching and learning in their schools.

2

Identify the Problem

Using Data to Transform Our Intentions

Some is not a number. Soon is not a time.

—Dr. Donald Berwick

In 2004 Dr. Berwick, CEO of the Institute for Healthcare Improvement (IHI), addressed a crowd of doctors and health care workers at a conference. He declared from the podium that his methods—if implemented—could save 100,000 lives over the course of 18 months (Heath & Heath, 2010). His mission was hospital and health care reform. From his work in and around the medical community for over 40 years, he knew that medical care errors in hospitals led to needless deaths every year. The data were evident and people in the profession knew the need was real. But how do you get doctors and health care workers to admit and identify mistakes in hospital care? They are already doing the best they can. Sometimes the only thing needed is a challenge, a push, and a system of support to help people improve—that was where Dr. Berwick came in.

Dr. Berwick didn't stop at problem identification. He confronted the issue of hospital care reform by proposing a challenge. During his address at the conference, he told the crowd of doctors and hospital administrators that his organization over the course of several years had identified and developed health care strategies that improved the effectiveness and efficiency of hospital care. In other words, implementing systems his staff designed would save lives and drive down costs. Offering consulting services to hospitals free of charge, he estimated 100,000 lives could be saved across the country within 18 months if the strategies were implemented.

Spurred on by a mother's story of a medical error that cost the life of her daughter, the doctors and hospital administrators in the crowd that day were moved to action by the Berwick challenge, and several hospitals joined the 100,000 lives campaign immediately. They welcomed outside support to improve their systems. In the end 3,103 hospitals participated in the campaign, and an estimated 122,342 lives were saved. The estimated number had an accuracy range of plus/minus 2,074 and was determined upon data analysis completed by three independent groups. Most of these lives were saved through simple techniques and practices in health care that Dr. Berwick's team implemented through training in each hospital that participated (The Governance Institute, 2006).

In April of 2010, Dr. Berwick was nominated by President Obama to be the administrator of the Centers for Medicare & Medicaid Services. Needless to say, his ability to identify problems and implement solution strategies delivered results in the field of health care, and he was recognized and rewarded for his efforts. It is not difficult to see the connection between Dr. Berwick's passion for patients and the work being done with data teams in schools. He began by identifying the problem and proceeded by implementing solutions based upon data.

■ TOOL 2: IDENTIFY THE PROBLEM

This tool is best used as an initial way for staff to identify their perception of what is occurring with a troublesome area. Using this tool is a great first step to identifying a problem a data team, individual, or school is trying to solve. Though identification is an important first step, it is also critical for staff to express how they feel about the problem. Connecting emotions to problems makes the data personal, and data that are personal have a greater chance of being addressed because feelings become attached to the numbers. In school as well as in life, it is often not a lack of knowledge or skill that prevents people from solving their problems; it is a lack of motivation and the will to do it. Many reform efforts are sound in theory but fail during the process of implementation.

Other reflection questions that need to be asked when using this tool are related to having staff think about the data that address the problem they're facing and the need to identify what those data are telling them. The final question addressed by this tool is a simple one that asks what they will do about it. Though this tool does not determine a course of action, the reflective nature of it gets team members talking about what to do next, and those courageous conversations yield seeds of change for powerful solution strategies.

Identify the Problem is a reflection tool (see Tool 2 on page 124 for a blank version to photocopy). Reflection is a great first step in helping staff to think about a problem they are facing, review data they have that address their problem, and ponder an action they can take to address it. This tool is helpful to generate the action steps and energy to address complex problems that do not have clear solutions or clean data. It can be completed individually, by teacher teams, or by an entire staff. Still another option is to have individuals complete the tool and compare their responses with others. This approach results in lively conversation.

Using Data to Unpack the Problem of Mobility

Lebanon, Oregon, is a semirural community in transition. Built upon the logging industry of the previous century, Lebanon is a town of 15,000 people situated on the western side of the beautiful Willamette Valley—the grass seed capital of the world. The rural landscape surrounding Lebanon consists of several thousand more people who send their children to one of Lebanon's eight public schools. Though the town's future is moving toward education and medicine with the arrival of a new medical school in the fall of 2011, the past was built upon blue-collar jobs that didn't require more than a high school diploma to obtain and provide work for a lifetime. Those days are gone for the most part, and the transition has been difficult for many people and families. As a result, all of the schools post poverty rates of over 50% and at some of the schools over 80% participate in the federal free and reduced lunch program.

The reality of what seemed like the constant movement between the schools caused many leaders in the school system to have serious concerns about student mobility. They questioned what could be done to mitigate mobility effects upon student learning and achievement—especially when the schools had different curricula, standards, and expectations. They started asking questions. The first questions posed were exactly how many students were entering the district, leaving the district, or moving around the district throughout the year? Records were analyzed, and the district began tracking the movement of every student on a massive spreadsheet. Throughout the course of the 2009–2010 school year, it was discovered that 648 students left the district, 625 students entered the district, and 748 moved around the district. If the same student moved more than once, each movement was counted. When the dust settled at the end of the year, 2,021 students had moved in, out, and around the schools—which represented a mobility rate of over 50%.

Poverty and mobility rates are linked hand-in-hand across the country. The more depressed a community, the higher the school mobility rates are. Anyone who works in schools knows that each movement disrupts the learning and relationship building process. Since each of the schools had different report cards and standards on which the reports were based, getting those report cards aligned became priority work for the school year. This problem was identified simply because leaders looked at the data around mobility and decided to do something about it. The district then implemented common formative assessments throughout the year to measure the universal standards. This action alone helped students transitioning in and out of schools throughout the year.

Reflecting on the mobility problem in Lebanon using Identify the Problem would look like Figure 2.1.

Figure 2.1   Identify the Problem (Example): Student Mobility in Lebanon

1. What problem are you facing?
The student population (4,000 students) is highly mobile (especially at our highest poverty schools). The mobility creates learning and relationship gaps for our students as they move in and out of schools.
2. How do you feel about it?
The student movement is frustrating for staff as they lose relationships with students and parents frequently throughout the school year, and it seems to have an academic impact upon student achievement and learning.
3. What data do you have about your problem?
We know that over 50% of our population is mobile. One third is moving in, one third is moving out, and another third is moving around the district.
4. What is your data telling you?
It is telling us that mobility impacts student learning and achievement. Our schools with the highest mobility are also historically the lowest achieving.
5. What will you do about it?
We need to develop a common report card across all of our schools, adopt a common curriculum, develop common formative assessments, and communicate horizontally across the district to make sure key content standards are being addressed in similar time frames.

Vertical Alignment and Mobility

After analyzing horizontal mobility among schools, district and school personnel started thinking about vertical mobility. They wanted to know the effect on grades and attendance of students who had experienced movement from school to school over the course of their career. They analyzed every high school transcript and individually asked students at the high school how many schools he or she attended throughout his or her career. The range went from two schools (since there are three K–8 schools in the district) to 12 schools. It was discovered there was not a discernible effect in grades or attendance among the students who attended two to four schools throughout their careers, but when a student was in five schools, and especially when they hit six schools or more, achievement and success (in terms of classes passed, grade point average [GPA], and attendance) plummeted. The data revealed something else as well.

The district had a tradition of awarding high school credit in eighth grade for students who were advanced and completed a course of study that included ninth-grade curriculum. In theory, this practice sounds like a great opportunity. In reality, the transcript study revealed several unintended consequences. For starters, many students who were awarded credit for core classes in middle school stopped taking those core classes later in high school once they achieved the minimum credits they needed to graduate. They were not thinking long-term and preparing for college or career. They were thinking short-term and looking for the easiest route out of high school. As a result, when they became seniors and thought college might be in their future, they scored extremely poorly on the SAT, ACT, and other college placement exams. Many of them would have scored higher in the ninth or tenth grade as opposed to the twelfth. They literally lost options for their future because they stopped taking challenging coursework in core areas after they reached the minimum requirement.

Another unintended consequence of this policy was the lowering of high school GPAs. More than any other number assigned to students in high school, the GPA sticks. Reflecting on this data revealed that the majority of students had higher GPAs *without* the credits earned in eighth grade. Several students lost the opportunity to be valedictorian in high school or graduate with honors because of credits and grades earned in eighth grade. Student responsibility and maturity plays a significant role, in addition to skills and intelligence, when it comes to earning grades. These unintended consequences were discovered only through asking questions about the data and reflecting on the answers.

Digging into data with questions, in order to identify the problem you are trying to solve, helps data teams avoid unintended consequences. Once problems are discovered, practices can be improved and policies changed. As a result of this data analysis, it is now rare in Lebanon Community Schools to offer high school credit in middle school. Instead, extensive advanced coursework within the curriculum grade span is offered so that student thinking and skills are constantly challenged, and opportunities for every student to grow and thrive are enhanced.

Using Identify the Problem in a Classroom

A third-grade teacher used Identify the Problem to help her think through how to serve a group of students in her classroom who were reading one and one-half years behind grade level. By asking herself the five reflective questions, she was able to identify some actions to take to help these students catch up to their grade level. Her reflections are captured in Figure 2.2.

Figure 2.2   Identify the Problem (Example): A Group of Students Not Making Progress in a Third-Grade Classroom

1. What problem are you facing?
The problem I am working on is a group of students in my class who are reading one to two years behind grade level, and only one of them is on an IEP.
2. How do you feel about it?
I feel strongly that these students need to make good progress this school year. As the school year progresses, I am beginning to feel more and more stress and concern because they are not making the progress I would like to see.

(Continued)

Figure 2.2 (Continued)

3. What data do you have about your problem?
I have STAR reading assessment (a reading assessment system by Renaissance Learning) score data, tested about every six weeks, beginning in September. I have Easy Curriculum Based Measures (CBM) data, and I have state test results.
4. What are your data telling you?
The data are telling me that the students are far behind grade level in reading and have not been making adequate progress to catch up to their grade level this year.
5. What will you do about it?
First, I think I will develop a questionnaire for the students to get their ideas about reading—what they like about reading, what they don't like, what is difficult, the best part of reading, and how much they read at home—to see if they have any ideas about how they can make their own reading better. I think I will sit down with each student and ask these questions so I can get more honest feedback. Next I will look at the reading instruction they are getting—how many minutes of the core, what kind of interventions, what seems to be working, and what can be done better.

Data Reflection Helps Budget Woes

How to do more with less resources is a problem nearly every public school and district in America is currently facing. Using the Identify the Problem tool was extremely valuable in helping an Oregon district with recent budget difficulties. The last decade in public education has seen the rise and fall of several budget cycles. In many places around the country there has been a lot more falling than rising. Falling behind only Michigan as the state with the worst unemployment rate during the recession that began in December of 2007, public school funding in Oregon has not done well in the last decade. In the midst of constantly rising employee costs and the costs of goods and services, Oregon's funding per student has declined over the last four years and is now less than $6,000 per student—one of the worst rates in the country. Schools are operating on less funding in 2010 than they were five years ago.

In May of 2010, Governor Kulongoski announced another across-the-board cut to education funding throughout the state due to lower than expected personal tax revenues from 2009 returns. School districts found themselves with a 5% budget cut that day, and that cut was followed by another 3% in August. An 8% cut does not sound like a lot, but when 75 to 85% of your budget is personnel, it feels more like 25%. The timing of the announcement couldn't have been worse. Most districts already negotiated contracts for the year and built their budgets. How would leadership respond to a crisis of this nature? The problem seemed simple enough. The budget was cut. The budget is mostly people. Time to start cutting people. One district resisted that temptation and instead began by identifying the problem they were facing. Problems of this nature are not unique to Oregon. A majority of states and districts across the country are experiencing budget shortfalls of one kind or another.

Because of a sense of urgency, the tendency in difficult, stressful situations is to try to solve problems with drastic measures before taking the time to study and understand them. Taking time as a team to identify problems with a few simple questions keeps staff from making knee-jerk, rash decisions that often result in more unintended consequences than the original problem they were trying to solve.

District leaders didn't want to think short-term at the local level—especially with budgets. They knew that no matter what the situation, great organizations try to think long term. Gathering together key administrative leaders in the district, they went through the Identify the Problem activity. By taking a few moments to write responses to the questions, the administrators were able to calmly share the data they had, how they felt about it, and what steps they felt should come next. Some of them realized that they didn't have nearly the data they needed so they couldn't even make a reasonable decision. Being able to stop and gather more data to afford a comprehensive review almost always leads to better decisions in the long run, and through the process, the problem is clarified so that it can be addressed effectively.

A Happy Ending to Budget Woes

Using Identify the Problem, the leadership team was able to come to a sensible decision that honored all stakeholders, treated staff with dignity and respect, and kept the best interests of the children and community at heart. Instead of responding to the governor's message with a knee-jerk layoff response, leaders realized that late spring was not the best time to make smart, long-term staffing decisions—especially when there were so many factors that influenced the budget still at stake, including enrollment, additional revenue forecasts, and future legislative action. Instead, the leadership team decided upon some quick across-the-board budget reductions in nonpersonnel budgets, came up with some creative ideas to reduce substitute costs, and strategically lowered the overall salary budget by 3%. The 3% reduction didn't have to be made up with immediate layoffs, but joint conversations enabled all stakeholders to work together to achieve the reduction collaboratively. Instead of dividing stakeholders, the problem brought people together in a proactive way.

IN THE FIELD: IDENTIFY THE PROBLEM

Figure 2.3 is a sample from a group of teachers who were in the midst of a climate problem at their school. Staff was starting to become polarized. Arguments, mistrust, a general lack of communication, and backbiting were on the rise. As a result, the school was becoming unhealthy and many staff members dreaded coming to work. Students were beginning to feel the stress of the situation as well and negative student behavior—especially bullying and harassment—was on the rise. The Identify Your Problem tool helped this team of teachers define what was really bothering them and come up with a course of action. By thinking through their problem, they were able to move past what was bothering them and become galvanized for action. When a team does not know what to do first, Identify Your Problem is a great tool to get team members talking, sharing, asking questions, looking at the right data, and moving in a positive direction.

Figure 2.3   Identify the Problem: Climate Concerns (Teacher Team example)

1. What problem are you facing?
The climate at the school is not positive. Seems like there are divisions developing among staff members. People are angry at each other and do not enjoy coming to work. Students seem to be acting out more.
2. How do you feel about it?
Upset and helpless. The school used to have a great climate, but it has changed in the last few years and gotten worse recently. We do not know what to do to fix it.
3. What data do you have about your problem?
Observations and conversations with staff. Survey perception data from staff, students, and parents. Data on student behavior—especially harassment—seem to be on the increase.
4. What are your data telling you?
Our perception is that the data are old. We only have a hunch (there is little evidence) that the increase in negative student behavior is connected to the climate issues among staff.
5. What will you do about it?
Meet with school and district administration to express our concerns. It might be helpful to conduct focus groups with staff to see if we can understand the root of the climate issue, and how extensive the problem is. Our schoolwide behavior team will need to review the student behavior referrals to see how the behavior can be addressed and if there is any connection to the climate issues. We need additional time to explore the problem further with leadership and come up with some positive action steps for improvement.

■ PUTTING IT ALL TOGETHER

Complex problems are not solved easily. Whether we are trying to figure out why Johnny isn't making progress in his third reading intervention, balancing shrinking budgets while increasing student achievement outcomes, determining how to address mobility, or strategizing how to reform public education, identifying the problem the team or individual is trying to solve is a critical first step in determining viable solutions that make sense and work in the long-term. All too often, we reach for a hammer when what we really need is a voltage meter. Unfortunately, when the only tool we have is a hammer, everything looks like a nail. Using a tool to identify the problem on an individual level through reflection and then sharing those perceptions with others in a team setting facilitates rich dialogue and through that dialogue, an array of sensible courses of action emerges.

When Dr. Berwick faced that crowd of doctors and hospital administrators with his challenge of saving 100,000 lives within 18 months, he put a number to the problem and identified a time to get it done. Being specific with data takes away all room for excuses and galvanizes people to a course of action. At the end of the day, everyone can measure progress, determine success, and set new goals, but it all starts with identifying the problem. Before a team can set aggressive goals that will take the organization in the right direction, it is necessary to identify the problem they are trying to solve. Dr. Donald Berwick was focused on saving lives through better health care. When schools are made better places for staff and students, the quality of life people experience is enhanced, learning soars, and minds flourish.

Lack of knowledge is not the biggest obstacle to improvement and better outcomes for students. Nor do we lack an understanding of what great systems look like or how to get there. Aside from resources in some contexts, the biggest obstacle is a lack of cooperation among stakeholders. Being able to identify problems together and work toward common solutions is the reform work of this decade that will successfully propel us into the next.

3

The Three Guiding Questions

Making Instruction Work

*Conversations have the capacity to promote reflection,
to create and exchange craft knowledge, and to help improve the
organization. Schools, I'm afraid, deal more in meetings—in talking and
being talked at—than in conversation. So how do we transform talk,
meetings, agendas, and posturing into conversation?*

—Roland Barth (2001, pp. 68–69)

Every July the world in France stops for the most well-known bicycle race on the planet, the Tour de France. Similar to the Super Bowl in popularity around the world and commonly known as *The Tour*, the race grabs the attention of many nonbicycle enthusiasts. The race is special because it is both grueling and intriguing. Never the same course twice, each year the racers must traverse the French countryside in multiple stages, while their times for each stage determine their placement in the overall race. Spectators from around the country and world converge each July in France to watch the month long drama unfold.

What makes the race unique is the fact that though there is an individual winner, no one can win the race alone. Teammates dedicated to each other must work together throughout each stage to support their champion. If an individual pulls away from the pack, he is quickly tracked down by the others and brought back. However, if a band of racers move forward as a group, the pace of the whole pack increases. The race is on.

The power of data teams doesn't come from test scores and graphs. It comes from questions posed by team members. It comes from bringing people together and initiating sustaining conversations that culminate in staff and student learning. Just as in the Tour de France, to be successful, teammates must work together so members of data teams can successfully collaborate and keep the goals of school improvement and student success ever present as the ultimate endpoint.

■ DATA AND CONVERSATION

Data without conversation yields little change or improvement. A data team can transform talk, meetings, agendas, and posturing by asking the right questions. Reflection—thinking and dialogue—are the trademarks of data-driven decision making. Data are not enough. Data must be discussed and reflected on. Asking questions is the best reflection tool available, and asking questions leads to meaningful data-filled conversations. It takes questions to get staff members beyond talking and being talked at. Questions engage the mind. They are essential.

The first questions data teams need to ask must focus on curriculum—what they will be teaching. Defining what is to be taught in terms of clear learning targets is central to the learning process. If we want to move beyond random acts of improvement, it begins with clear learning targets that students and staff understand, accept, and work toward with a laserlike focus.

The breakthrough work of Richard Dufour around professional learning communities (PLCs) is best summed up in an article he wrote in May of 2004 for *Educational Leadership* (DuFour, 2004) entitled, "What is a 'Professional Learning Community'?" In this article, DuFour states every professional in the learning community must engage in three crucial questions that drive the work of PLCs:

1. What do we want each student to learn?

2. How will we know when each student has learned it?

3. How will we respond when a student experiences difficulty in learning?

For our third data tool (see Tool 3 on page 125 for a blank version to photocopy), we focus on these questions and expand them to include the concepts of learning targets and the importance of providing extension activities for students who meet the learning target.

■ TOOL 3: THREE GUIDING QUESTIONS

The Three Guiding Questions tool points reflection in a direction that leads to better conversations and solid improvement in achievement data. Since the goal is to impact learning and help every child to reach his or her full potential, teachers need tools that help them think about the work they are providing to their students and opportunities for sharing and discussing that work with each other.

If a teacher is able to skillfully answer these questions for her students, classroom instruction improves. If a horizontal team of teachers (similar grade, course, or department) works on these questions together, an entire grade level improves. If a vertical team of teachers (one grade before and after each level) ask and answer these questions together, the entire school improves. If schools across the district work on these questions together, the entire district improves. These questions, combined with collaboration and a focus on results (DuFour, 2004), are the formula for obtaining significant gains in student learning and achievement.

Question 1: What critical knowledge and/or skills (learning targets) does each student need to have or be able to perform during this unit/course of study?

Standards alignment and the power standard movement has helped address this question for many educators, but often those documents and exercises do not create measurable learning targets for students that are clearly communicated, implemented, and supported in the classroom. Teachers must, first as individuals and then as teams, come to consensus about clear learning targets and communicate those targets to students in many different ways so that the targets are valued and owned at the student level. As standards change over time, they must continually be reviewed to ensure they are aligned to local and state assessments.

With the advent of the Common Core (currently adopted by 42 states), the majority of the country is involved in analyzing state standards over the next few years to determine what students should learn and when they should learn it. The Common Core emphasizes rigor and high standards with the goal of each student being ready for college and career upon graduation from high school. You can download Common Core standards and learn more about this national reform movement at *www.commoncore.org*.

Question 2: How will we know when each student has learned it?

The second essential question of PLC work focuses on assessment. There are many sophisticated ways to assess student learning and progress toward clear targets, but the most effective and basic way is often overlooked—checking for understanding. As teachers provide clear instruction, they should be checking for understanding all along the way by asking questions, having students raise their hands if they know answers, restating the objective to the class or in small groups, and reflecting through writing. Informal formative assessment begins by checking for understanding but there also must be a system of formal assessment to measure progress toward the learning targets.

As far as formal assessment is concerned, it should be meaningful to the student and measure the learning target being assessed. Assessments can be open-ended response papers, multiple choice tests, essay questions, authentic performances, projects, or demonstrations of learning. They should be scored on a rubric. The key is that the assessment—whichever one is used—is *common*. In other words, each teacher addressing the agreed-upon learning target uses the agreed-upon assessment tool. Why is this so important?

Data have little value for school and district improvement if they cannot be shared beyond an *n* of one. If teachers all have their own learning targets, assessments, and rubrics, data teams and PLCs are of little value. The lack of a shared focus leaves little to look at and learn from collectively. The whole point of creating data teams is to develop a forum of professionals who examine student performance on common assessments and/or rubrics that address meaningful learning targets and have conversations around the student work that comes from those assessments. This creates the conditions under which instruction is most likely to change and improve. State assessment tests force this conversation to some degree once a year, but they do little to change instructional practice because the assessment is developed outside of the classroom and may have varying degrees of staff ownership.

Over the next five to ten years this will most likely change as national assessments are designed to measure progress and achievement toward the Common Core. Many states that have adopted the Common Core have also joined a consortium to design an electronic test that will be used for assessing student attainment of the standards. The consortium with the most potential and gaining the most participation (30 states) is called the SMARTER balanced assessment. Funded by the federal government, this test is slated to be piloted during the 2014 to 2015 school year and promises to deliver computer-adaptive assessments, open-ended performance tasks, and computer-based formative tools that provide feedback to students and teachers about progress prior to the final spring summative assessment. To learn more about the SMARTER balance assessment, visit *http://www.k12.wa.us/smarter/*.

However, authentic student learning in the classroom increases even more if teachers get solid feedback about learning targets they design attached to assessments they develop. Therein lies the power of data teams. The purpose of data teams is not to conduct an autopsy of state assessment results once a year sorted into a dozen demographic configurations. The real purpose of data teams is to facilitate conversations about student performance based upon common targets so that teachers can learn from each other and improve instruction in the moment—when the students are still in their classrooms. This is how we transcend state assessments. We raise the bar and point it toward something that matters to those being assessed. Unfortunately, developing rigorous common assessments requires time that many teachers do not have and systems do not provide. Time for teachers to work together in collaborative teams *must* be built into the workday or workweek. Without regular time to meet, data teams have little chance to change practice.

One organization taking action to support high school teachers in the development of rigorous performance assessments at the high school level is the Educational Policy and Improvement Center (EPIC). Dr. David Conley (2010), author of *College and Career Ready*, is the founder of EPIC. EPIC's work begins and ends with teachers in mind. Working with educators all over the country, EPIC has developed a battery of tools to support teachers in their design of work that matters, including complex course-ending tasks it calls College-Readiness Performance Assessment System (C-PAS). These structured tasks—developed by and for teachers—prevent busy teachers from having to reinvent the wheel when it comes to designing high-quality performance tasks to prepare students for college. These tasks extend all the way down to the sixth grade. Since most of EPIC's work was developed through federal grants, most of its resources can be downloaded at no cost at *www.epiconline.org*.

Question 3: How will we respond when a student needs intervention or extension along the way so that each one can reach (or exceed) the learning target?

Data fluency requires a deep commitment to monitoring progress throughout the learning process and providing support as needed. In order for all students to reach their full potential as learners, support must come in the form of intervention or extension. Students who are performing below the standard need intervention. They need additional, effective, and focused instruction to accelerate their learning. Students easily meeting or exceeding the standard need different activities to extend their learning and help them rise to the next level of achievement. There is always another level of learning that can be achieved. Schools and districts that settle for students meeting the standard might be doing as much damage as the ones that ignore and don't address achievement gaps. This condition is called the opportunity gap. Just because students can easily meet the standard does not mean they have been provided with the rigorous opportunities they need to reach their full potential as learners.

The third question focuses on more than progress monitoring. It addresses response. PLCs must not only develop systems to monitor student progress toward the defined targets through common formative assessments but also determine how to respond to the students who are not making progress toward the defined learning target or who have quickly surpassed it. This final question— though clearly the most complex—is also the most important because it is the only question that has the power to make adjustments in the moment that increase student learning in real time. It helps the team do something different in order to achieve a better result.

How to Use Three Guiding Questions

This tool can be used as a reflection exercise to help staff members think about the most important knowledge and skills they want students to learn in their classrooms. The knowledge and/or skills are best identified as learning targets. This tool also helps staff members to think through how they assess the critical knowledge and skills they have recognized and what they can do to provide intervention or extension activities for students in need of additional support. Individuals or teams can use this tool. It can be used to address a particular standard or target that students are not reaching based upon the state assessment, or teachers can use this tool when designing instruction from the ground floor up.

For maximum effectiveness, plenty of reflection time and meaningful conversations are required when using this tool. Teachers may find it helpful to access state and national content standards and/or curriculum resources in addition to state test results or local assessments when working with this tool. The questions should be answered in the order presented. Upon completion, teachers find it helpful to share their responses with horizontal and vertical teams. The goal, of course, is to reach agreement on a common rubric (if appropriate), along with common expectations, assessments, and responses to those assessments. This process impacts classroom practice. Student work that emanates from classroom practices produces the most critical testimonial to the usefulness of this tool.

Asking the Right Questions

Author Peter Block (2003) emphasizes if we really want to do what matters, we need to begin by asking the right questions. Are we focusing on the right things? Should we really be chasing test scores? If we really want to do what is best for students, then shouldn't the focus of our time and attention be on teaching strategies that result in student learning? How do we measure that learning? Proficiency-based teaching and learning—quality instruction—focuses on measuring learning through demonstration.

Local, state, and national initiatives and legislation in recent years have been driving public education toward student achievement outcomes—a worthy goal most easily measured by standardized test scores. However, are test scores alone the outcome we value most for our children? Or is it the process of measuring what matters, analyzing the data, and designing meaningful interventions and support that culminate in increased learning? Where does quality of experience stack up in the student learning equation? Educators intuitively know data outcomes derived from summative test scores are not what matters most. The collaborative sharing of student work around common assessments has the biggest impact on improving instruction and transforming classroom practices.

For most communities, higher test scores and student achievement outcomes are not enough. Great test scores without improved learning, thinking, and ultimately success in society is not the goal. What communities and families value is a focus on learning and making schools better places to be—increasing the students' quality of experience. It is time to start asking hard questions such as, "What is the difference between student achievement and school improvement, and is that difference important?" The past two decades of achievement focused initiatives still haven't reformed the K through 12 public education system. Racial and poverty achievement gaps still persist. Despite all of our efforts, we are still missing something.

■ THE POWER OF THINKING

In the end, there is no substitute for quality, and teaching students and staff members to think is the highest level of quality school leaders can hope to achieve in their schools. It is the job of educational leaders to help make schools better. Better for everyone, the staff members who work in the schools, the students who attend, the parents who send their children, and the community-at-large that benefits from well-rounded, educated citizens who are learners and thinkers prepared for life.

Staff members who focus on making their schools better (school improvement) see gains in student achievement. A new direction is emerging out of an old theme. Focusing on the needs of the whole child has a greater impact on student achievement than simply focusing on better test scores. If we want the best outcomes, we must focus on the right things, and we start by asking the right questions. There is a difference between student achievement and school improvement efforts that serve every child. That difference matters.

Student achievement is about outcomes—the end result upon which schools get judged. School improvement is about process. It is about the experience students have while they are in school. It is about the work teachers provide for students. It is about the design of their lessons. Are students reading? Are they writing? Are they talking about what they are learning? It is important to ensure that the work is of high quality and that it is meaningful. It should make students think. It should be hard. Are the students learning? If so, how much, and what are they learning? How do we know? These are the important questions that our third data tool addresses, and this is where exceptional PLCs invest energy through reflection. If the focus is on improving the process of learning using data, the end point is better results. If we can keep our focus and attention on the work that matters most, we will end up with better schools where all students experience quality learning every day.

Corbett: A District That Thinks

Ten years ago, Corbett School district, an average and ordinary rural high school located near Multnomah Falls outside of Portland, Oregon, got a new superintendent named Bob Dunton. He told his staff members to stop worrying about the tests and teach students to think. He told them the state standards were too low, and test results would take care of themselves if they taught students how to think and work hard toward higher expectations.

When Bob arrived, the school did not offer a single Advanced Placement (AP) class. AP courses are the gold standard for rigor in high schools across the country. Sponsored by the College Board (creators of the SAT exam), AP course syllabi must be approved by a governing board to appear on a student transcript. AP represents the most recognized standard for college prep courses in America.

Ten years later in June of 2010, *Newsweek* rated Corbett High School #1 in the state of Oregon and #5 in the country based upon the number of AP tests students take at the school (Matthews, 2010). The average graduating student at Corbett takes 11 AP exams during the course of his or her high school career. The school had more students who took AP courses and passed AP tests than anywhere in the state, and there are only 300 students in the school! The state test is an afterthought in Corbett because its standards and teaching are more rigorous than the state test. Corbett's standards are readiness for college and career through challenging coursework and supportive environments. These are average students with ordinary teachers doing extraordinary work. The school's academic decathlon team is number one in Oregon year after year. It competes and regularly defeats schools five to ten times Corbett's size. These things weren't happening ten years ago.

The Corbett transformation started with a conversation that quickly became a challenge to make students work hard and think. Dunton believed the average and ordinary students in his out-of-the-way high school were special and could compete with anyone in the country. It was simply a matter of will, determination, training, and fierce conversations. He initiated those conversations. He challenged the status quo, and over time his persistence paid off and a community was transformed. Belief with a vision is a powerful thing.

Conversation Promotes Thinking and Reflection

Real conversations are evidence of reflection. Susan Scott (2004) discusses the power of conversations in her landmark book, *Fierce Conversations*. The goal of a conversation is to uncover the truth and get to the real causes of why things are they way they are and then do something to make things better. Scott is famous for her quote, "While no single conversation is guaranteed to change the trajectory of a career, a company, a relationship, or a life, any single conversation can" (p. iv).

Consider the conversations you are having in your school. Are those conversations genuine? Do they matter? Are you getting to core issues that make a difference in the lives of students? Do those conversations promote high levels of thinking and reflection? Do they motivate your team to do something different? Are you using data to inform those conversations, and if so, how are you using it? Whose future are you changing today, and how are you changing it?

IN THE FIELD: THREE GUIDING QUESTIONS

High school staff members were working to align their standards and develop power standards for each of their classes. Teams of teachers had been meeting on a regular basis during collaborative time to work on these standards, but the work was slowing down and the exercise had become laden with effort that was not getting implemented or translated into improved instruction in the classroom. The Three Guiding Questions tool was used to get the school back on track by helping it to see the importance of identifying learning targets, coming up with common assessments, and then using formative student work to improve instructional outcomes. A horizontal team of ninth-grade language arts teachers explored something similar to the sample in Figure 3.1 in the early stages of the process and refined the teacher's common assessment through continuous collaboration to conform to clearly articulated work samples that not only addressed state standards in their field but also gave the teachers the professional freedom to use content they felt most appropriate for their courses. In the end, it was the sharing and scoring of student work based upon the common rubric that was the most helpful for improving instruction across classrooms.

Figure 3.1   Ninth-Grade Language Arts Course

1. What critical knowledge and/or skills (learning targets) does each student need to know or be able to do during ninth-grade language arts (1st Semester) course of study?

   a. Write an autobiographical narrative essay.

   b. Read, understand, and analyze the plot, characters, and symbolism of Romeo and Juliet.

   c. Present a persuasive speech using props, visual aids, and/or electronic media.

2. How will we know when each student has learned it?

   a. The narrative essay will be scored according to a common rubric. Students will be provided feedback on their essay at different points in the writing process.

   b. The Romeo and Juliet end of class assessment will assess the following skills: use of imagery, allegory, symbolism, sequence of events, main ideas, supporting details, characters, responding to major themes in the text and connecting those themes to the reader's experience. Quizzes at the end of major sections will provide formative data about each student's understanding of the text and skills to be assessed.

   c. The persuasive speech will be scored according to a common rubric. Students will receive feedback in small groups from their peers as they prepare their speech.

3. How will we respond when a student needs intervention or extension along the way so that each one can reach (or exceed) the learning target?

   a. Students struggling with writing the essay will have additional small-group instruction in the writing process.

   b. The teacher will reteach to the class literacy skills or concepts in need of extra instruction based upon the formative assessments. Students showing a high mastery of these skills and/or concepts will help with these presentations.

   c. Extra support for students who are struggling with their speech will be provided during the advisory period. Students possessing unique presentation aptitude will be provided opportunities to demonstrate their skills to the class.

Source: DuFour, 2004

■ PUTTING IT ALL TOGETHER

The most important component to influence instruction is not defining targets, picking an assessment, or determining ways to measure progress. The most important element is the sharing of student work that comes from this process in team settings. Quality instruction depends on a teacher's ability and will to deliver it, but like achievement in the Tour de France, no one wins alone. Effective data teams increase instructional quality because teachers are able to share with one another student work that emanates from common assessments. Collaborative conversations are the key to making progress. Targets, assessments, progress monitoring, and interventions/extensions are simply tools used to facilitate the sharing of student work and instructional strategies that lead to increased learning and achievement for every student.

4

Analyze Your Students

Let the Data Decide

Our brains are positive illusion factories.

—Chip and Dan Heath

In their best-selling book about change, *Switch*, the Heath brothers (2010) describe a human behavior phenomenon known in the world of psychology as *positive illusion*. Positive illusion describes why 90% of university professors consider themselves above-average instructors, most people consider themselves good drivers, and people keep buying lottery tickets despite the fact they are more likely to be hit by lightning than ever win a big payout. Through positive illusion we understand why middle school boys declare professional basketball player to be their first career choice with a plan of falling back on becoming a rock star if hoops don't work out.

Data help educators analyze possibilities and potential. It moves us beyond positive illusions by telling us the truth. Data help educators make better decisions—decisions that make sense. Not every college sophomore gets to drop out of Harvard to start Facebook and make billions of dollars, but there are millions of students who finish college every year and go on to have meaningful and fulfilling careers. Analyzing data keeps us grounded. It helps data teams make wise decisions that generate the results they are looking for and helps them to achieve cherished goals. It enables school staff members to move from hoping to planning, from being lucky to being strategic, and from losing to winning.

■ TOOL 4: ANALYZE YOUR STUDENTS

Data tool 4, Analyze Your Students (see Figure 4.1) shows how to analyze and sort your students based upon student need—no illusions or guesswork needed. Placing students into these four categories is the most effective way for members of a data team to quickly see where each of their students is at compared to a common standard:

- Blue: significantly above the standard
- Green: at or above the standard
- Yellow: below the standard
- Red: significantly below the standard

In a healthy educational system, 80% to 85% of the students should be in the green and blue zones. It is difficult for any system to respond effectively if more than 20% of the students are below the standard and in need of intervention support. If a school and classroom has over 20% of its students in need of intervention based upon a benchmark assessment, the instructional core provided to all students must be examined, analyzed, and improved. Strengthening the core is job number one for schools and classrooms that fall below the 80% threshold.

Teach to the Top

Districts across the country are implementing a *teach-to-the-top* approach to core instruction. The evidence of achievement-gap-closing schools and districts demonstrates that targeting core instruction to the top third of the class yields the greatest improvements in the least amount of time. Targeting instruction to the top third of the class not only challenges all students' growth effectively but also helps the middle and bottom thirds of the class to make the greatest gains. Students on each end of the continuum (the exceptionally high and low) need additional support and instruction regardless of what pace the class is traveling.

The color-category method of analyzing students can be used for any single set of data. It can be used for high schools that want to analyze failure rates, GPA, or attendance. It can be used for middle schools studying student behavior, state assessment results, or formative local assessments. Basically, all one needs to start sorting students into categories of need are numbers and a standard. Whether one starts with the standard or with the numbers simply depends on what the data team is trying to improve. Some areas have well-established standards. It is easy to start with the percentage of freshmen who are failing classes because there is no need to establish a standard in that case. However, if your district does not have a common standard to describe effective writing, then one will have to be developed before students can be analyzed and sorted into categories of need.

In the brave new world of performance-based assessments where schools and districts are taking on the challenge of redefining what failure means and what it looks like, new standards will need to be developed. Educators are starting to

Figure 4.1 Analyze Your Students (Example)

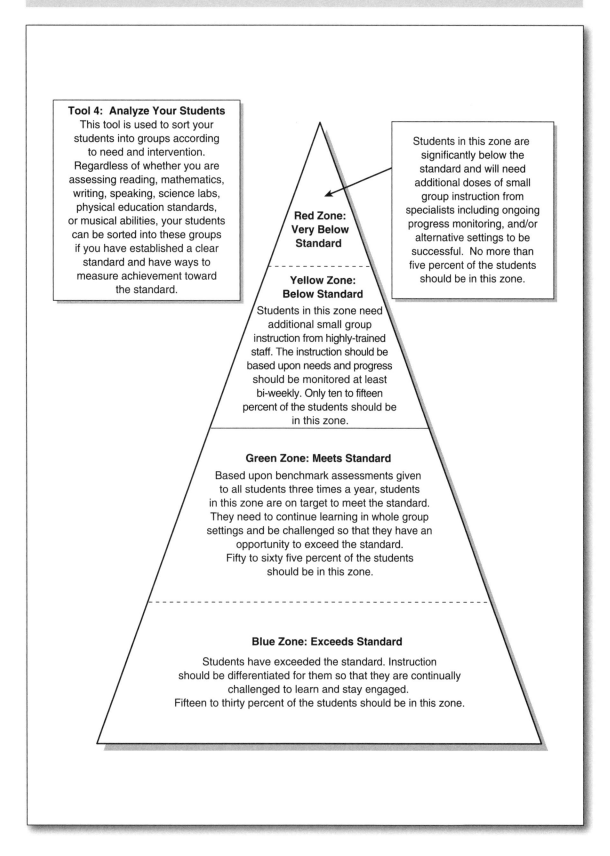

Tool 4: Analyze Your Students
This tool is used to sort your students into groups according to need and intervention. Regardless of whether you are assessing reading, mathematics, writing, speaking, science labs, physical education standards, or musical abilities, your students can be sorted into these groups if you have established a clear standard and have ways to measure achievement toward the standard.

Students in this zone are significantly below the standard and will need additional doses of small group instruction from specialists including ongoing progress monitoring, and/or alternative settings to be successful. No more than five percent of the students should be in this zone.

Red Zone: Very Below Standard

Yellow Zone: Below Standard
Students in this zone need additional small group instruction from highly-trained staff. The instruction should be based upon needs and progress should be monitored at least bi-weekly. Only ten to fifteen percent of the students should be in this zone.

Green Zone: Meets Standard
Based upon benchmark assessments given to all students three times a year, students in this zone are on target to meet the standard. They need to continue learning in whole group settings and be challenged so that they have an opportunity to exceed the standard. Fifty to sixty five percent of the students should be in this zone.

Blue Zone: Exceeds Standard
Students have exceeded the standard. Instruction should be differentiated for them so that they are continually challenged to learn and stay engaged. Fifteen to thirty percent of the students should be in this zone.

realize that 59% looks a lot different than 30%, yet both percentages traditionally result in a failing grade for a student. Helping teachers design grading systems based upon proficiency-based thinking—designing systems that support what we know about teaching, learning, and motivation in the 21st century—requires us to adopt new standards before we can sort and analyze students by need.

Analyzing Driving Quantitatively

So how do we use quantitative data analysis to help us move past positive illusions? Since quantitative data help us to see, we see things in it that grab us and jar us into action. Let's go back to the driving example. About 80% of American drivers state they are above-average drivers. Obviously, if we took 100 drivers and ranked them on a scale from one to 100, 80% of those folks would not be above average. But instead of ranking all of these people on a curve from best to worst, what if we defined what constituted good driving? What if we analyzed the attributes of good drivers and determined that good drivers don't speed, don't get angry, don't tailgate, and do obey road signs? It would be relatively easy to collect and track data on those concrete, observable measures. From that data, one could create a standard for good driving. According to that standard, it would be possible for 80% of the drivers in America to be qualified as good. We could also qualify drivers as in need of improvement or bad based upon the data collected. Creating the standard is the first step to analyzing your students.

■ CREATING THE STANDARD

Most elementary teachers serving primary students today are familiar with a popular measure for reading success—oral reading fluency. Extensive research has demonstrated that students who are fluent readers score better on reading comprehension assessments, and since reading comprehension is the foundation of state and national reading tests, building a student's fluency should help him or her perform better on local, state, and national assessments. And, of course, doing well in reading also has a positive impact on a student's sense of self-esteem.

Fluency and understanding are increasingly important at the secondary level where students are supposed to be reading to learn as opposed to learning to read. With each progressive grade at the secondary level, students are asked to read more content in their textbooks, and they are required to read more variety of texts—everything from nonfiction technical texts (science), to nonfiction instructional texts (social studies) to problem-solving texts (math) to literacy texts (language arts). High schools need to assure student success by preparing students who struggle to read with strategies that develop fluency, comprehension, and thinking. Fluency matters, and students who are not fluent will most likely struggle throughout their school and adult careers. Years of research with tens of thousands of children has created benchmarks (standards) to measure where students should be in the fall, winter, and spring of each school year so that schools know whether their students are on track for success in oral reading fluency through eighth grade.

A research-based system developed by the Center on Teaching and Learning (CTL) at the University of Oregon has developed a vast array of materials to support early reading and has established benchmarks and learning targets that districts and schools can use to see if their students are on track to become successful readers. Information about CTL and its work with DIBELS (a measurement system to assess early literacy) can be located at *https://dibels.uoregon .edu/.* More recently the CTL developed another system called Easy Curriculum Based Measures (CBM) that districts can use not only to assess reading fluency but also reading comprehension, vocabulary, and math. Demonstrations, access, and free accounts for Grades K through 8 to the Easy CBM tool can be found at *www.easycbm.com.* Built on the foundation of fluency measures, Easy CBM adds measures of comprehension and vocabulary to the reading data and provides an overall score for whether or not a student is on track as a reader or in need of additional interventions.

Similar to DIBELS, the fluency portion of Easy CBM can be administered by any trained adult in a one-on-one setting. The comprehension and vocabulary components are administered using a computer. The web-based program includes progress monitoring and database software that tracks the data entered for each student during the benchmark assessments and has a built-in progress monitoring component that enables staff members to track the progress of students who are placed in intervention groups to make sure the chosen intervention is having the desired effect on student learning.

Measuring to a Standard

Once a standard by which students can be measured is established, analysis of student results can occur. The first question to be asked is very simple: Did the students meet the standard? This is a yes or no question that places students in one of two categories. The second question is similar. For the students in the *yes* category, were they a strong yes or a weak yes? In other words, are they significantly above the standard or simply at the standard? Students exceeding the standard should be provided additional learning opportunities so that their potential can be maximized. Students at the standard should be challenged so that they also can exceed the standard.

Students below the standard also fall into two categories. They are either close to the standard (a weak no) or significantly below the standard (a strong no). Interventions must be provided to these students to help them reach the standard. A menu of effective interventions must be provided for those students who are below the standard, and how far a student is behind the standard should determine the frequency and intensity of those interventions. Interventions should always be in addition to the core instruction that all students receive. One of the biggest mistakes that can be made—a mistake that will actually increase achievement gaps—is to pull students who are behind out of core instruction and give them interventions instead. The research and evidence is crystal clear. Schools that close achievement gaps provide core instruction to all students, and students who are behind get additional instruction, not replacement instruction.

The Kennewick Model

Kennewick school district in Washington is a leader in the movement of creating common assessments, measuring students according to those assessments, and then applying a host of strategic interventions as necessary. Its story is documented in the book *Annual Growth for All Students and Catch-Up Growth for Those Who Are Behind* (Fielding, Kerr, & Rosier, 2007). This book explains how the district was able to close achievement gaps across the district by effective reform and coordinated system design from the ground up. The strategy was simple but effective. Provide excellent core instruction for all students and additional, targeted instruction for those students who are behind. Set your goals. Measure your progress. Report your progress, and keep moving forward with focused intention.

Decision rules based upon data must be used to help determine how to provide support for all students. If the goal is helping each student to become college and career ready, school staff members must do everything they can to help students reach their full potential as thinkers, learners, and problem solvers. Just meeting benchmarks, especially in states where the benchmarks are relatively low, is not enough. Until we have a high national standard consistent for all, there will always be variance between states and grade levels that must be considered.

Analyzing Students in Local Districts

Springfield Public Schools *(www.sps.lane.edu)* use a reading model that places students into the four categories based upon the data they gather through the Easy CBM assessments. Developed by reading coaches, principals, and district administrators and teachers, this assessment tool has guided schools in their decisions to provide support through a Response to Intervention (RTI) model. Implemented and perfected over the last ten years by practitioners and researchers in the Tigard-Tualatin school district *(www.ttl.k12.or.us)*, the needs of each student are tracked and monitored by well-trained and equipped data teams. A menu of interventions is provided for small groups of students and closely monitored to provide the maximum growth for each one.

At Cascades Elementary School, data teams meet by grade levels to frequently review data gathered from benchmark and progress monitoring assessments and to design specific interventions for students who are behind and need additional support. In the fall of the 2009 to 2010 school year, nearly half of the school's students were placed in the yellow and red zones according to benchmark assessments. By the spring, that percentage was reduced to under 20%. In many schoolwide title programs, like Cascades Elementary, where mobility rates regularly reach 40% to 50%, monitoring students and providing support is absolutely essential to their success. Schools like Cascades can close gaps and raise the bar of achievement for all because they are committed to solid core instruction, benchmark all students through common assessments, provide interventions for those who are behind, and monitor the progress of students assigned to those interventions.

Classroom Example

A first-grade teacher was participating in a research grant through the University of Oregon called Enhancing Core Reading Instruction in First Grade (ECRI). In this highly structured program, teachers learn to use a variety of protocols to help students improve fluency and comprehension outcomes. Student progress is monitored with a variety of assessments. The teacher used the Analyze Your Students tool to see what kind of progress her students were making throughout the intervention. More information about the ECRI project can be found at *http://ctl.uoregon.edu/research/projects/ecri.*

Using the data tool and Easy CBM assessments, she discovered that within the course of three months her students went from 52% meeting the standard to 73% meeting the standard, and even more remarkable, the percent of students in the red zone dropped from 29% to 9%. She also discovered that the Harcourt Quick Mastery Theme test (Houghton Mifflin Harcourt, n.d.) correlated to the results she was seeing from the Easy CBM assessment. It became clear to her that what seemed in the beginning to be a rigid, scripted program was actually very helpful for many of her students, and their growth in reading was appearing on a variety of assessments. Using the data in this way helped change her practice in the classroom, resulting in strong improvements for her students.

IN THE FIELD: A KINDERGARTEN SUCCESS

Benchmark assessments, progress monitoring, and specific interventions worked for the kindergarten reading program at Riverview elementary school. In the fall of 2009, Riverview staff members assessed all of their students with the Easy CBM reading assessment. When they analyzed the results, they discovered 81% of their students were not meeting the standard and in need of progress monitoring, intervention, and support (see Figure 4.2). The students were not ready for kindergarten. Since it was impossible to intervene with so many students, the teachers got busy strengthening core instruction. They devoted additional time to reading. They incorporated more skill-based lessons into their group instruction. They increased the rigor and pace of core instruction and used frequent assessments to guide their instruction. Fortunately, the district provided full day kindergarten—a necessity in these days of high-stakes accountability. With additional time, focus, attention, and interventions for those students who were the furthest behind, the teachers were able to make adequate growth for every student and catch up growth for many. By the end of the school year, 80% of the district's students were at or above the standard (see Figure 4.3).

Figure 4.2 Analyze Your Students (Example): Fall

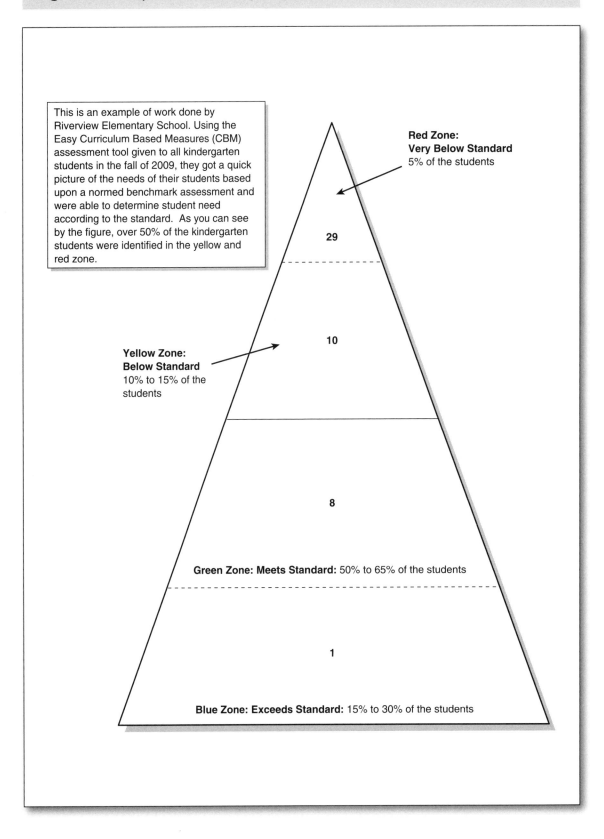

This is an example of work done by Riverview Elementary School. Using the Easy Curriculum Based Measures (CBM) assessment tool given to all kindergarten students in the fall of 2009, they got a quick picture of the needs of their students based upon a normed benchmark assessment and were able to determine student need according to the standard. As you can see by the figure, over 50% of the kindergarten students were identified in the yellow and red zone.

Red Zone:
Very Below Standard
5% of the students

29

Yellow Zone:
Below Standard
10% to 15% of the students

10

8

Green Zone: Meets Standard: 50% to 65% of the students

1

Blue Zone: Exceeds Standard: 15% to 30% of the students

Figure 4.3 Analyze Your Students (Example): Spring

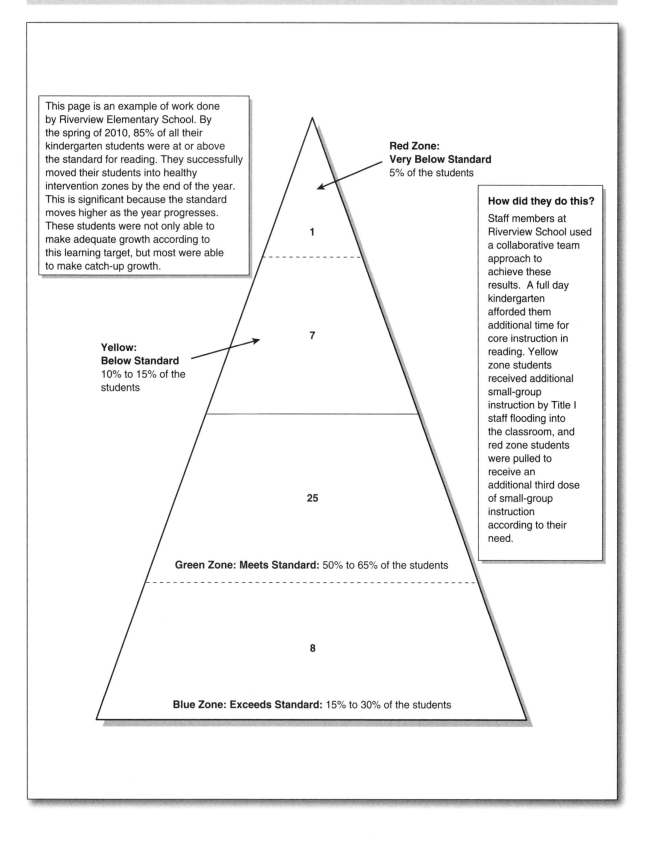

This page is an example of work done by Riverview Elementary School. By the spring of 2010, 85% of all their kindergarten students were at or above the standard for reading. They successfully moved their students into healthy intervention zones by the end of the year. This is significant because the standard moves higher as the year progresses. These students were not only able to make adequate growth according to this learning target, but most were able to make catch-up growth.

Red Zone:
Very Below Standard
5% of the students

How did they do this?
Staff members at Riverview School used a collaborative team approach to achieve these results. A full day kindergarten afforded them additional time for core instruction in reading. Yellow zone students received additional small-group instruction by Title I staff flooding into the classroom, and red zone students were pulled to receive an additional third dose of small-group instruction according to their need.

Yellow:
Below Standard
10% to 15% of the students

1

7

25

Green Zone: Meets Standard: 50% to 65% of the students

8

Blue Zone: Exceeds Standard: 15% to 30% of the students

■ PUTTING IT ALL TOGETHER

It is not only possible but also necessary for teachers, grade-level teams, schools, and districts to analyze student data in terms of individual need according to a standard. This is the heart of continuous improvement. The Analyzing Your Students tool is simple to understand and relatively easy to implement. The most difficult component of this tool is identifying the target and having the discipline to assess that target on a regular basis. Once a target has been identified and a standard has been established, the physical work of sorting your students into categories of need is an extremely powerful experience for staff. Once needs have been identified, the work of determining intervention strategies and taking action with those strategies is much easier.

In his last book before his death, *A Game Plan for Life*, legendary coach, teacher, and mentor John Wooden described how he learned his philosophy for taking action from his college basketball coach, Piggy Lambert, who emphasized that the team which took the most actions—and often made the most mistakes—would be the team that would eventually come out on top (Wooden & Yeager, 2009, p. 59). By focusing on doing something differently based upon the information around them, his teams were able to constantly adjust, learn, and score more points.

By taking the time to analyze your students before you take action, positive illusions can be eliminated and your data team will avoid the unintended consequences that befall schools and districts that rush from one initiative and intervention to another in the quest for the holy grail of test score improvement. Lasting results don't happen that way. There are no shortcuts. Sustained improvement is result of consistent, targeted, and effective effort over time.

5

Four Quadrants

Creating Crosshairs With Data

*Either you are the drama of your everyday life or you are seeing
the world as it is. These are the choices; you can't have it both ways.*

—Seth Godin (2010a)

There is nothing more intriguing, interesting, or captivating than a good conspiracy theory. However, beneath the layers of drama that seem to connect on the surface, most of those conspiracy theories prove false. Reflecting on data helps individuals get beneath the surface of the drama—to see the world as it is and do something about it, or in the words of blogger Seth Godin (2010b), "to make a dent in the universe." Data tools help us to effectively dig beneath surface conspiracies and prejudices. They help us to understand. They help us to learn, grow, and be better.

The Four Quadrant tool is used to analyze the relationship between two sets of data. Any two data sets can be studied. The goal is to see the relationships that exist between the two data sets and make decisions based upon the patterns and results. Four quadrants are formed by creating a low to high continuum with each of two sets of data. The intersection of these two continuums creates four quadrants. Figure 5.1 is an example of how to display the relationship of urgent work and important work in the Four Quadrants framework.

TOOL 5: FOUR QUADRANTS: ■ CREATING CROSSHAIRS WITH DATA

Quadrants have been used to analyze data for years. In Stephen Covey's (2004) landmark book, *The Seven Habits of Highly Effective People* Covey uses four quadrants to discuss how effective people spend their time. Figure 5.1 shows how the continuums of urgent work and important work intersect according to Covey's research and work with highly effective people.

45

Figure 5.1   Covey's Four Quadrants of Highly Effective People

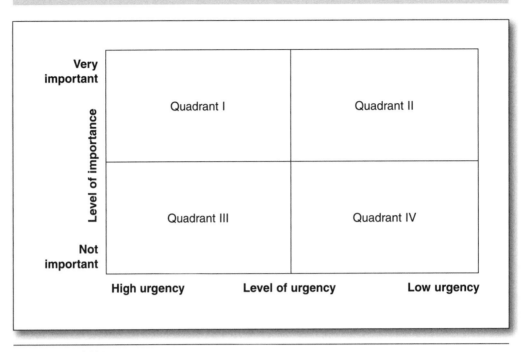

Source: Covey, 2004

To illustrate in Covey's framework, highly effective people spend a great deal of time in Quadrant II doing important work that is not urgent and as little time as possible in Quadrant IV doing not important work that is not urgent. In school districts, Quadrant II work for superintendents would include visiting schools, building partnerships with key community organizations, and serving on the local educational foundation board. It might include redesigning the district's website to make it more user-friendly or reading books about how to improve the organization. Quadrant II work for a principal would include visiting classrooms, attending conferences with teacher teams, or using a data tool with the site council to understand the most recent PSAT scores for the school. It would also include making home visits (when a student isn't in trouble) to build relationships and gain trust with parents and community or conducting surveys to understand student, parent, and staff perceptions.

In Quadrant III one finds leaders spending too much time composing long e-mails when a simple sentence would do the job just as well or writing detailed required reports and planning documents that no one reads, uses, or values. Teachers in Quadrant III assign worksheets that keep students busy and quiet, but the work assigned doesn't promote learning or thinking. Quadrant II teachers have their students write and share what they write. Writing is thinking on paper. There is no substitute. They have their students ask questions and create classrooms where students are constantly thinking and demonstrating what they know and are able to do.

Quadrant I can be nicknamed the *crisis corner*. It includes helping the senior who needs one credit to graduate find the right class to take or problem solving with the irate parent whose child just failed ninth-grade English with no record that the teacher informed the parent that failure was a possibility. For the district office it includes solving a host of employee related problems and conflicts that must be dealt with immediately. Organizations or leaders that move from crisis to crisis don't get better. They get frustrated.

Quadrant III holds court to urgent matters that are not important, such as completing required reports. Hundreds of hours are spent completing required reports every year. It is urgent work that must be done. Deadlines are attached, but it is not very important, and very little of it helps a school actually improve. However, these reports may be tied to funding, and therefore it is urgent work that must be done.

Though Covey's four-quadrant framework seems simple enough, it can be very enlightening for individuals, teams, or schools that use it to analyze how they spend their time. For instance, if a professional learning community (PLC) spends the majority of its precious time discussing details of the upcoming field trip, that Quadrant III activity (urgent, not important) gets in the way of taking the time to look at the most recent student fluency scores and determining how to regroup students for instruction (important and not as urgent, Quadrant II).

In the world of school finance, district staff members who take the time to budget their plan (as opposed to planning their budget) effectively operate from Quadrant II (important, not urgent). They operate from vision and priorities so when a money crisis arises they are calm and collected. As a result, they make smart decisions. District staff members who plan their budgets poorly generally operate in Quadrant III (urgent, not important), cycling between feast and famine and spending money based upon who shows up at the budget hearing.

The problem is that the pace of school and life constantly pulls us away from Quadrant II. A lot of people are subconsciously stimulated by the drama of crises, and some people are good at manufacturing them so that they have something urgent to do. It takes discipline and leadership to spend time on Quadrant II tasks because there are always mandatory reports to write, a crisis to deal with, and e-mail to answer. The next time you are in a meeting that you feel is going nowhere and perhaps driving you crazy, draw two intersecting lines and begin tracking the amount of time being spent in each Quadrant. You might be surprised by what you find.

Reeves's Four Quadrants: Lucky, Leader, Loser, and Learner

Education reformer Doug Reeves uses four quadrants to help school teams analyze whether they are moving in the right direction with school improvement with his four *L* framework. Published in his book, *The Learning Leader*, Reeves (2006) uses four quadrants to explore two data sets: results and adult actions/attitudes. Reeves's four quadrants are labeled Lucky, Leading, Losing, and Learning. His framework is represented in Figure 5.2.

Figure 5.2 Reeves's Four *L* Framework for School Improvement

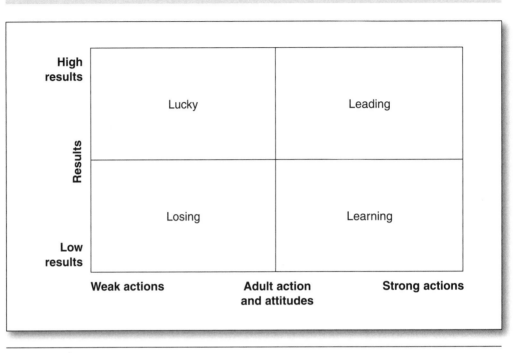

Source: Reeves, 2006

In this framework, school staff members look at a result they are achieving. If the result is high achievement in comparison to other schools with similar demographics (above state and district averages), then the question is What adult actions and attitudes were in place when these results were achieved? For instance, strong adult actions and attitudes would mean that all adults in the school believe all children can learn at high levels, that staff members collaborate regularly around data and use that data to improve instruction, that their instruction is aligned with standards, and that they are providing challenging work that requires students to think. There are a host of ways to gauge adult actions and attitudes—anything from perception surveys and interviews to observations (learning walks) and assessments. School and district assessments that measure adult actions and attitudes toward implementing Response to Intervention (RTI), a system that focuses on the prevention of roadblocks that hinder academic or behavior learning, can be found under the evaluation tab located at *www.pbis.org*.

Schools that fall into the lucky quadrant are ones achieving great results, but that can't articulate or point to the specific adult actions and attitudes that caused those results to occur. In other words, the results have more to do with the school's address and demographics than effective teaching. Reformer Tony Wagner describes the lucky quadrant in his most recent best seller, *The Global Achievement Gap* (Wagner, 2010).

In this sobering exposé, Wagner documents the results of hundreds of learning walks through some of the high schools in America with the best test scores.

In these suburban havens, he was hoping to find excellent teaching that inspired students to learn and excel. What he found instead—and explains in painful detail—are listless, bored students going through the motions to earn points and grades. He also found satisfied teachers relying on the students' innate abilities and social advantages to continue posting great test scores. In other words, in Wagner's assessment of those American schools he visited, the lucky quadrant had a lot of residents, perhaps not as many as in the losing quadrant but definitely more than in the learning and leading quadrants. According to Wagner, only 1 out of 20 classrooms he visited exhibited rigorous, high-level instruction that made students think.

In the four *L* framework, losing schools are those who have weak results and no evidence that the adults are behaving and believing in ways that align with best practices. In these schools, unfortunately many of which are located in urban centers across the country, one will most likely find high levels of minority students, along with high rates of poverty, English language learners, and student mobility. These schools frequently show up on lists of schools not making average yearly progress (AYP) and cycle through improvement efforts that yield little results led by well-meaning adults and reformers committed to closing the achievement gap but somehow not being successful at it.

School staff members in the learning quadrant have weak results, but learning walks in the school reveal the adults are acting in ways that promote learning and achievement. In other words, they have identified agreed-upon standards for instruction and have developed learning targets for those standards along with assessments beyond state tests to measure progress toward those targets. They look at student work together, watch each other teach, adjust instruction based upon their data, and work collaboratively in horizontal and vertical teams. These activities represent hard work, and they require consistent and considerable effort over time to become perfected. Learning schools become leading schools through the refinement, application, and institutionalization of these reforms.

Using the Four Quadrants to Gauge RTI Progress

The Four Quadrant tool can also be used to chart a school or district's progress in implementing RTI. Effectively implementing an RTI model requires a school to be fluent in their use of data and application of standards. Using those two elements as a guide, a four quadrants implementation road map looks like Figure 5.3.

Using this framework as a road map the four quadrants can provide guidance to schools and teams about which activities to focus on as they implement a system that supports effective instruction. The goal of RTI lies in Quadrant II— effective intervention. Schools that effectively intervene change their whole-group instruction based on agreed-upon learning targets, common assessments, and the data that come from those assessments. They also monitor and adjust their small-group and individual systems of support and work for all staff members to provide effective interventions. Unfortunately, many schools and districts attempt to design intervention systems before they have done the

Figure 5.3 RTI Implementation Road Map

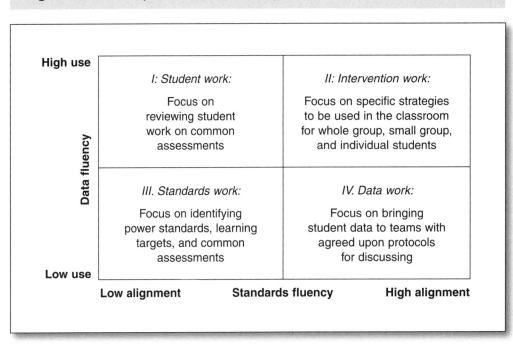

standards work and data work necessary so that the intervention work is effective. These shortcut approaches where schools and districts rush to intervention programs before they have done the deep standards and data work eventually lead to *initiative fatigue* where schools hop from bandwagon to bandwagon looking for a quick fix to their problems. It takes consistent time and effort to advance to Quadrant II, and it only occurs through the crossroads of data fluency and standards expertise.

Most schools in need of improvement are not fluent in their data, and staff members have not agreed upon power standards, adequately defined learning targets, or determined what common formative and summative assessments they will be using. This is Quadrant III work, and it is the starting place for all PLC, RTI, and data teams that want to make a difference. Downloading state standards at a particular grade level is Step 1. Analyzing those standards together in grade-level teams, identifying which ones are the most important, and deciding upon learning targets is Step 2. Step 3 is aligning available curriculum to the learning targets, and Step 4 is determining which common formative and summative assessments will be used to gather data so that improvements can be made based on these data over time. Step 5 is vertically aligning the standards, targets, and assessments to one grade level above and below. All of this work should be done in teams. It takes time and effort, but once it is accomplished, data can be gathered that are practical, important, and used to intervene and improve instruction in a variety of contexts (whole group, small group, and individual).

Schools and teams that have spent the necessary time determining power standards, learning targets, and assessments can operate in Quadrant IV, gathering data that matter and taking time to look at it with data tools to help them be fluent with the data. Data fluency is measured by the ability to analyze and use data to determine what to do next (effectively intervene).

Teams fluent in data use and systems but unsure of how their curriculum connects to power standards and learning targets start in Quadrant I by looking at their data in conjunction with student work, paying particular attention to evidence of power standards and learning targets. Knowing how to effectively intervene is dependent on becoming familiar with standards, learning targets, and common assessments. Hence, these need to be articulated even if staff members are familiar with data and how to use it.

Using the Four Quadrants to Analyze Classroom Data

The Four Quadrants can also be used by individual teachers to analyze any two sets of student data. The four quadrants can be used to look at student attendance and grades, attendance and behavior, grades and behavior, or reading comprehension and fluency rates. Using this framework to analyze data can provide keen insights about the next intervention to try in the quest to improve instruction and student learning. Figure 5.4 illustrates what can be learned by looking at reading comprehension and fluency rates with the Four Quadrant tool.

Extensive research indicates there is a strong correlation between reading comprehension and fluency (Fielding, Kerr, & Rosier, 2007). In other words, students who understand what they read are generally fluent. However, when students are learning how to read, or when they are struggling to learn how to read, using the Four Quadrants to measure progress is a great strategy to see which students are on target and which students need more support. This particular analysis has been conducted (with different scales) from first grade up to juniors and seniors in high school. Often there are more struggling readers at the high school level than one suspects. As students get older, they learn coping

Figure 5.4 Analyzing Reading Comprehension and Fluency

	High	
	I: Students in this quadrant understand what they read, but read slowly. An additional intervention in fluency is needed.	II. Students in this quadrant read fast and understand what they read. No additional interventions are needed.
Reading comprehension	III. Students in this quadrant read slowly and do not understand what they read. They need additional fluency and comprehension interventions.	IV. Students in this quadrant read fast, but don't understand what they read. An additional intervention in reading comprehension is needed.
	Low	
	Low fluency Reading fluency High fluency	

strategies to mask their inability to read well. They can pass their classes with average or even above-average grades, but they are not reading very much on their own, and as a result, their reading does not improve. While survival strategies can work in many high schools, students who rely on them do not fare well in college, which is one reason why only 55% of students who start college obtain a degree within six years. Measuring comprehension and fluency throughout high school and providing interventions to support those students who function below the baseline can be a vitally important strategy for creating lifetime readers ready for college and career.

■ CLASSROOM EXAMPLE: THIRD-GRADE CLASSROOM DATA IN FOUR QUADRANTS

A typical third-grade classroom analyzed using comprehension and fluency would look like Figure 5.5. Individual students (indicated by an *x*) are placed into the four quadrants according to their reading comprehension and fluency skill.

In Figure 5.5, the reading fluency scale (*x*-axis) runs horizontally from left to right with 20 words per minute on the left side of the continuum and 200 words per minute on the right side. In this illustration, the fluency baseline at third grade is 120 words per minute. The vertical–axis measures reading comprehension according to an RIT scale. The RIT scale is used for the Measures of Academic Progress (MAPs) assessment that provides a comparative measurement tool of reading comprehension for students in Grades 3 through 12. More information about this assessment and how to use it used can be found at *http://www .nwea.org/products-services/computer-based-adaptive-assessments/maps.*

Figure 5.5   Analyzing Reading Comprehension and Fluency: Third Grade

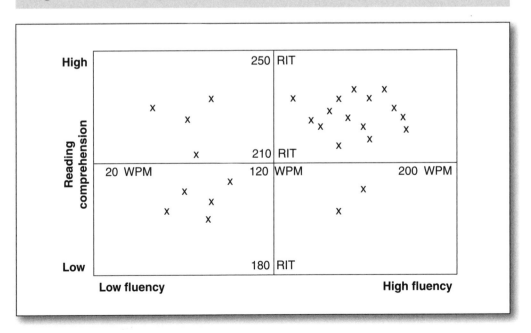

Similar to grade-level comparisons, the advantage of an RIT scale is the ability to see where a student is on the scale at any point in time. For instance, a third grader can score a 240 on a third-grade test, and a high school student can score a 240 on a high school test. However, each score would communicate something different to us about what the student needs. A score of 240 in third grade tells us the student is advanced and needs more challenging work throughout the day, and a score of 240 in high school tells us the high school student is on track to graduate (236 is the high school graduation standard). A score of 240 on a third-grade test does not signal that the student is ready to graduate (since the content tested was third-grade content), but it would signal that the student is on track to exceed graduation standards and should be receiving above grade level work.

Using the Four Quadrants to plot data relationships for individual students enables teachers and teams of teachers to compare two sets of data and graph those data into quadrants so that decisions can be made regarding which intervention to use and when to use it. With this visual tool, teachers can quickly come to decisions based on data about what to do to support their students in the learning process.

In Figure 5.5, the Four Quadrant tool provides keen insights for the teacher regarding how to structure small-group reading and which students need to be in which groups. All 26 students need whole-group instruction, but some of the students need additional interventions. For instance, a student who understands what she reads, but reads slowly (lack of fluency) needs a different intervention than a student who is fluent but doesn't understand what she is reading.

The four students in Quadrant I need a fluency intervention. The two students in Quadrant IV need a comprehension intervention, and the five students in Quadrant III need both. The teacher can group the students in Quadrant I and III (nine total) and provide a fluency intervention to that small group. The students in Quadrant IV and III (six total) can also be grouped and provided with a comprehension intervention. In this way, the students who are behind in comprehension and fluency each get an additional intervention according to their needs (double dose), and the students who are significantly behind get a triple dose of reading instruction. All of this can occur with the teacher only needing to set up two additional small groups. The Four Quadrants can also be helpful for teams of teachers to analyze grade-level data, school-level data, or even district-level data.

Using the Four Quadrants to Analyze Grade-Level, School-Level, and District-Level Data

A grade-level team of teachers can use the Four Quadrants to assess how every student is doing in his or her grade level to help make instructional decisions about which students need additional support and how to deliver that support. Teams can look at comprehension and fluency across grade levels, the relationship between grade point average (GPA) and attendance, or reading test scores and GPA, or math and writing test scores. The possibilities are endless.

The only limitations are time and purpose. Once a teacher or team of teachers decides what they are trying to achieve, it is simply a matter of finding two data sets that provide the most pertinent information about how to improve in that area.

■ TEACHER AND PRINCIPAL EFFECTIVENESS IN FOUR QUADRANTS

Educator effectiveness has become the national conversation. Communities, institutions, and individuals around the country are looking at ways to measure and monitor educator effectiveness because of the importance and value of a quality teacher in the classroom and an excellent leader in the school. There are many shortcut models currently in vogue that seek to link test score data to effectiveness. Technology can be used to create teacher and principal *credit scores* that link multiple standardized measures (tests, surveys, and observations) to effectiveness ratings. Many of these models do not generate excellence in the classroom. Excellence comes from the pursuit of perfection coupled with effective coaching, support, and resources. Education is not an individual sport, and almost every effectiveness rating system on the market places individuals on a bell curve and ranks them accordingly.

However, there is a way to use the Four Quadrants to measure teacher and principal effectiveness based upon two sets of standards. A Four Quadrant approach supports data teams and builds great schools, which is not achieved through individual ranking systems. Figure 5.6 shows how principals fall into the Four Quadrants based upon measurement in 14 standards divided into the domains of instructional leadership and building management.

Figure 5.6 Principal Effectiveness

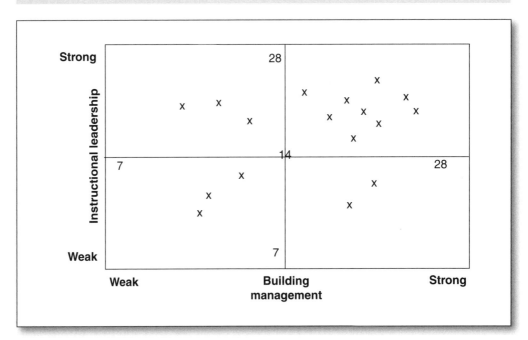

In this framework, each principal is evaluated on 14 standards from a scale of one to four according to the domains of instructional leadership and building management (Hess, 2011). The assessment range of this measurement tool is 7 to 56 (based upon a maximum rating of four and a minimum rating of one on each standard). Charting the value each principal receives provides keen insight into the type of support and training needed to improve the performance of individuals or small groups. Support teams can be formed to provide needed skill development in the areas assessed as weak.

Instructional Leadership Standards for Principals

- Knowledge of curriculum: Understanding the essential components of effective curriculum design to ensure that it is relevant to the students
- Knowledge of instruction: Ability to identify the skills of masterful teaching and use the power of relationships to support effective classroom instruction
- Knowledge of assessment: Understanding the connection between standards, rubrics, and formative and summative assessments and how to use that information to improve curriculum design and instruction
- Powerful teaching and learning: Ability to making the work relevant, rigorous, and supportive
- Vision: Ability to articulate a clear and compelling vision to galvanize staff members to engage in the difficult work of school improvement
- Data-driven decision making: Bringing data into every context, setting, and improvement effort, resulting in student achievement
- Innovation and continuous improvement: Thinking outside the box to drive change and improvement of all outcomes

Building Management Standards for Principals

- Professionalism: Responds in a timely manner to all requests and engages effectively in meetings with all stakeholders.
- Building operations: Maintains and supports clean, well-maintained facilities
- Effective systems: Ensures building systems operate smoothly so that all stakeholders know what is expected of them and how to get the support they need to be successful
- Positive relationships: Builds and maintains positive relationships
- Community connections: Is visible, available, and communicates to build trust with the community and all stakeholders
- School climate: Creates and maintains a strong and positive school climate that supports students and staff
- Cultural diversity: Values and supports everyone

In this researched-based evaluation model, each standard has three to four clearly defined performance targets, and there is a corresponding descriptive rubric in narrative form that goes with the standards so that feedback can be specific and helpful. Adding components to the evaluation process that include staff surveys on the standards, principals assessing their own performance, goal setting, observations, and digital portfolios designed for principals to demonstrate their competency on the standards makes the evaluation process a 360-degree experience with the most potential for growth.

Teacher Effectiveness in the Four Quadrants

In a similar vein, teacher effectiveness can be analyzed using the Four Quadrants. Figure 5.7 demonstrates the evaluation of teachers in the two domains of classroom observations and dialogue, conversations, and artifacts. There are eight standards in each of these domains, so the range of assessment in this framework would be eight to 32. Placing a group of teachers into the Four Quadrants based upon their performance on the standards would look like Figure 5.7.

A distribution of this nature communicates that teachers are scoring higher on the classroom standards (instruction with students) than in the nonclassroom standards (planning, preparation, and professionalism). Reflecting on these data gives district administrators and principals insight into what additional training and support is needed for teaching staff, and it also helps to calibrate assessment strategies for principals. For more information about either of these evaluation assessment tools and how they can be used to provide meaningful feedback, e-mail robhess@comcast.net or visit the Lebanon Community Schools webpage at *www.lebanon.k12.or.us.*

Figure 5.7   Teacher Effectiveness

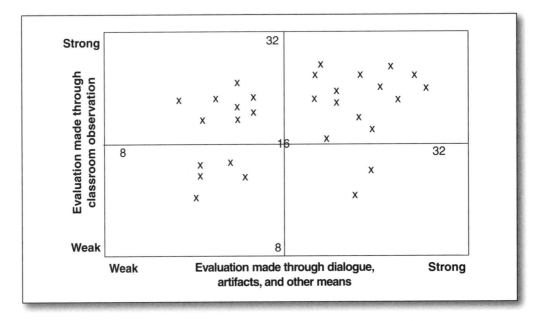

Classroom-Based Instructional Standards
(Evaluated through classroom observations)

- Knowledge of content: The teacher demonstrates a deep understanding and expertise of content knowledge.
- Knowledge of students: The teacher understands the background information of the students and uses that knowledge to support learning.
- Instructional goal setting, objectives, and implementation: The teacher understands and communicates learning targets and works with the students so they know the learning that is expected of them.
- Climate of respect, engagement, and high expectations for learning: The teacher maintains and prioritizes high expectations for engagement, respect, and learning in the classroom environment and experience.
- Classroom procedures and physical environment: The teacher structures the classroom in such a way that students clearly know, own, and follow classroom procedures, and the classroom space is effectively organized to support authentic engagement and self-directed learning.
- Managing student behavior: The teacher actively keeps students on task and prevents off-task behavior with verbal and nonverbal cues, movements, and a host of activities/strategies.
- Lesson delivery: The teacher's lesson delivery is fast-paced and concentrated.
- Feedback to students: The teacher gives students consistent and constant feedback on their behavior and academic performance.

Non-Classroom–Based Standards
(Evaluated outside of classroom observations)

- Curriculum design: The teacher designs curriculum that is relevant, rigorous, aligned to standards, and communicated horizontally and vertically.
- Assessment, monitoring, and follow-up: The teacher has a system for assessing student learning and monitoring progress.
- Using data and assessment to inform instruction: The teacher grows in data fluency that includes gathering the data and using it effectively to improve instruction.
- Ongoing professional growth: The teacher is committed to ongoing professional growth that includes job-embedded training, coursework, reading, and attending conferences.
- Professionalism and availability: The teacher acts in a professional manner that includes availability and working well with others.
- Communication: The teacher knows how to effectively communicate with other staff members, parents, and community partners.
- Commitment to instructional initiatives and programs: The teacher is able to support the building and district improvement initiatives.
- Special education requirements: The teacher is able to work effectively with other professionals to meet the needs of at-risk students.

IN THE FIELD: ANALYZING FRESHMAN FAILURES

The key to preventing high school dropouts is addressing the freshman failure rate. According to the most recent data available across the county, 40% of high school freshmen fail at least one class. Should we be shocked when only 60% of high school students graduate in four years? The numbers are strikingly similar. A high school wanted to improve its graduation rate so it focused on addressing the freshman failure rate. The school started by creating freshman cohorts with shared teachers. It added a support class each day for all students to help them with their core classes. A year and a half after these supports were in place, the freshman failure (D, F, Incomplete) rate at the school decreased from 38% to 26%. All of the school's hard work only moved the number 12%. It was a start, but the school didn't make the progress it was looking for. It needed to get to the next level, so it turned to the Four Quadrant data tool for help and had a group of seniors work with the data in their statistics class.

The school took the list of every freshman who earned at least one D, F, and Incomplete grade and placed these freshmen in the Four Quadrants based upon two sets of data: reading skills (based upon the state test) and attendance. It looked for patterns and started asking some questions. It also started getting some answers. The school discovered that student attendance had a greater impact on student failure than a student's reading skill. With this information in hand, the school used the Four Quadrants to explore attendance and work completion and discovered that the work completion rate was the biggest predictor of student failure.

With this new knowledge, the next intervention the teachers tried involved examining the work they provided. They focused on how they could make the work they assigned to students more engaging and meaningful. They also worked on their systems of communication with students. How could they deliver better feedback on work completion to students? How could each teacher hold their students more accountable for work completion? What policies could be developed to support work completion and attendance? How could they prevent students from not completing the work? They put in place individual and group goals for students that targeted work completion. By the end of the semester, these additional interventions lowered the freshman failure rate from 26% to 15%. They achieved a breakthrough result and are continuing to make progress that results in more students graduating from high school.

■ PUTTING IT ALL TOGETHER

As you can see, the Four Quadrant tool has a variety of uses to help educators reflect on their data and find patterns so that they can effectively intervene. The key to making this tool work is knowing what needs to be improved and then determining two variables to explore. This work can be done by individuals who simply want to explore and improve their own classroom data, by students who want to explore how to solve a problem, or by a data team or PLC focused on school improvement outcomes. Using data in this way is one of the secrets to being able to *make a dent in the universe*. With the Four Quadrants, a team can harness group intention and unleash self-imposed accountability and ownership for improvement that can be sustained over time.

6

Wagon Wheel

Using Multiple Points of Data to Drive Instruction

Every man must decide whether he will walk in the light of creative altruism or the darkness of selfishness. This is the judgment. Life's most persistent and urgent question is, What are you doing for others?

—Martin Luther King, Jr.

In January of 1957, in the wake of the successful nonviolent Montgomery Bus Boycott, a group of 60 African American ministers met to discuss the next steps in the civil rights movement. Dr. Martin Luther King, Jr. was present at the meeting. The group convened with the goal of forming an organization to coordinate and support nonviolent direct action as a method of desegregating bus systems across the South. The group eventually formed the Southern Christian Leadership Conference (SCLC) and named Martin Luther King, Jr. as its first president.

The early days of the SCLC were full of passion and spirited debates. There were many leaders calling for swift and radical action to end the blatant discrimination throughout the South. Some of the leaders were advocates of fighting the inequities with violence. Others were not. Dr. King had a remarkable skill for pulling divergent people together around a single idea. He believed that the use of nonviolent protest was the most powerful force for addressing injustice. As a result, he galvanized the participants into a unified course of action. In 1959, he went to India to study Gandhi's techniques of nonviolent resistance, and in that same year, he decided to move back to Atlanta to assume leadership of the SCLC and help make the organization a national force.

Dr. King's ability to listen intently to the conflicting and passionate voices around him and make decisions that solidified groups of diverse thinkers is one of the reasons he was the most successful civil rights leader of his generation. The Wagon Wheel (Figure 6.1) can be thought of as a sophisticated listening tool. It is best used to decipher between wide ranges of data inputs and lead a team to a unified course of action.

■ TOOL 6: WAGON WHEEL

The Wagon Wheel is the last of the quantitative tools. Since the Wagon Wheel enables data teams to look at complex and multiple data sets at the same time, it often opens up understanding and insight into data that the team members thought they already knew and understood. It can be used to discover patterns, look for clues, or track progress over time for a particular initiative. The Wagon Wheel as a data tool can be found in the work of Stephen White (2005) from *Show Me the Proof*. It is a deep reflection tool designed to help mine deep understanding to perplexing problems. Edward Deming (1986) also used the Wagon Wheel in his work with Japanese companies in their quest for quality and in the rebuilding of their society in the aftermath of World War II.

When using the Wagon Wheel as a data tool, each spoke represents a set of data. Label each spoke according to the data you are trying to measure. Look for patterns in the data to explain the results and to determine what actions to take next. The Wagon Wheel is a very powerful tool for understanding and predicting outcomes. Figure 6.1 illustrates the use of the Wagon Wheel and the implications for enhancing student learning.

■ MAPPING FOURTH-GRADE WRITING ON THE WAGON WHEEL

Figure 6.1 illustrates the mapping of one district's 2009 fourth-grade writing results on a Wagon Wheel. The percent of proficient writers in fourth grade as defined by the state test is charted onto each spoke of the wheel. The district average and state average are also represented. When district leaders and principals looked at these data, there were some immediate *aha's* and courses of action that surfaced. According to Reeves (2006) and many others, writing is the most important and transferable skill when it comes to college entrance and success. Next to reading, college students spend more time writing than any other academic skill. Writing is thinking on paper, and being able to write effectively opens doors of opportunity for student scholarships and success in college.

Revealing these data in the Wagon Wheel format immediately caused district leaders to begin a districtwide writing initiative that is still going on today. Activities have included the use of schoolwide writing prompts, increasing the number of writing work samples, an emphasis on writing every day and in every subject, training on how to score writing according to a rubric for teachers who did not formally teach writing, analysis of student writing by teams of educators in order to discover ways to improve the

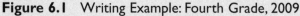

Figure 6.1 Writing Example: Fourth Grade, 2009

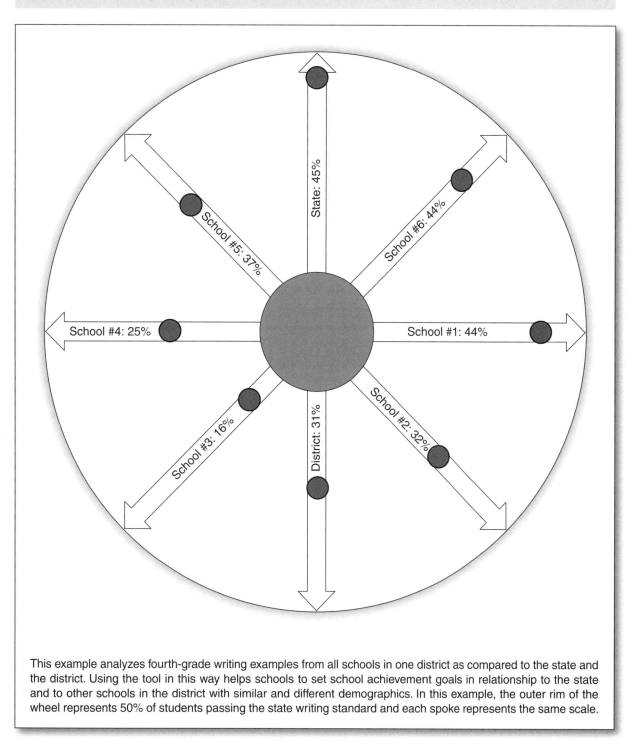

This example analyzes fourth-grade writing examples from all schools in one district as compared to the state and the district. Using the tool in this way helps schools to set school achievement goals in relationship to the state and to other schools in the district with similar and different demographics. In this example, the outer rim of the wheel represents 50% of students passing the state writing standard and each spoke represents the same scale.

teaching of writing, and adopting a districtwide curriculum that authentically engages students in writing every day.

A second influence of the Wagon Wheel was that each school's faculty members began examining how they were teaching writing in their building. Since there was a wide range of writing scores in the district (anywhere from 16% of students passing to 50%), difficult questions needed to be explored.

Once it was determined that subgroups had little impact on these data (schools with high mobility and poverty outperformed other schools), it was evident that instruction needed to be examined. During that examination, it became clear there were some differences in how writing was being taught at each of the schools and how writing was assessed on the state test.

When making instructional decisions about data, it is important to know what the data are measuring. The state writing test primarily measures a student's ability to write a five-paragraph essay. While being able to organize one's thoughts into a five-paragraph essay is an essential skill, obviously there are many more writing competencies involved in being a proficient writer. In Figure 6.1, analyzing the data led data teams to an intense examination of writing instruction for the five-paragraph essay at the fourth-grade level and a related discussion regarding foundational writing skills and additional writing competencies.

■ REFLECTING ON THE DATA

Figure 6.2 is a Wagon Wheel that represents both 2009 and 2010 fourth-grade test scores in those same schools. What do you notice? Obviously, the increased emphasis in writing across the district yielded some direct improvements at the fourth-grade level. There was a 14% difference between the state and the district in 2009 at the fourth-grade level. The gap closed to a 6% difference in 2010. Two of the schools improved significantly—school number six and school number four. At the same time one school *decreased* significantly (11%), and another, who was already the lowest at 16%, barely improved to 17%. The Wagon Wheel approach visually illustrates an array of data, and in doing so, can quickly provide data teams with information they can use to examine patterns and ask questions that ultimately lead to improvement strategies.

Were you curious about how each of these cohorts of students did in reading and math in the 2009 and 2010 school years? For instance, did school number four just have a smart cohort come through in 2010 (or a slow one go through in 2009)? How can we seek to answer that question? Charting the math and reading scores of each school in 2009 and 2010 gives us some insight into the question.

Did you generate a question inquiring about the writing skills of students when they entered the fourth grade? The data in Figure 6.2 are summative data scored by the state department. One might ask, How would these same students do on a formative assessment given and scored by teachers in October or November? One might also be curious about whether these teachers calibrated their scoring with the state scoring. Did they determine interrater reliability across teachers within the same school? Using an approach that collaboratively engages teachers in analyzing formative data can lead to powerful action planning that culminates in significant improvement in summative data.

Are you curious about what the teachers at school number four (strong improvement) did differently in 2010? Do you wonder what they say contributed to their improvement? What do the students say? What about the school

Figure 6.2 Writing Example: Fourth Grade, 2009 and 2010

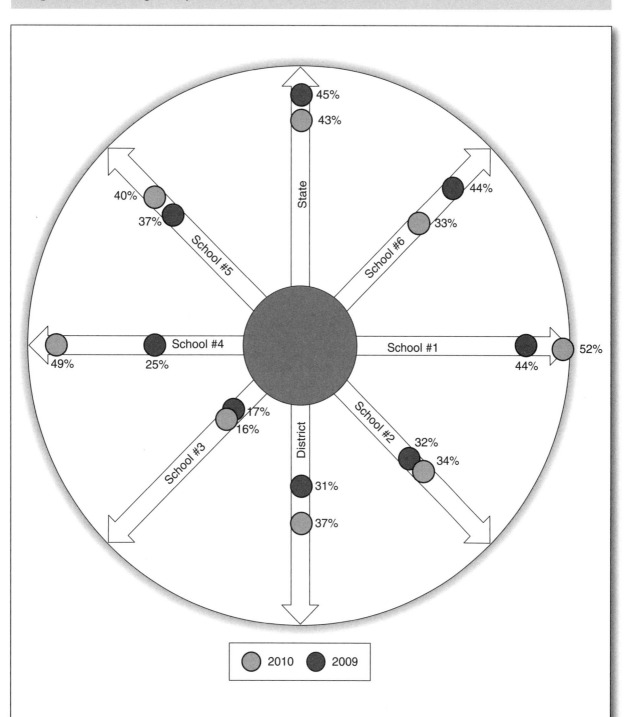

This example analyzes fourth-grade writing examples of all schools in one district as compared to the state over a two-year period of time. Using the tool in this way helps schools to set school achievement goals in relationship to the state and to other schools in the district with similar demographics. In this example, the end of the wheel represents 50% of students passing the state writing standard and each spoke represents the same scale.

that decreased? What questions would you ask the teachers, principal, and students of that school? What would you ask the teachers of the school that has been underperforming?

As Figure 6.2 illustrates, the Wagon Wheel is a great tool that teams can use to generate questions about their data, and when teams become curious about their data, instructional changes and breakthrough results are right around the corner. Now let's take a look at another year of data in Figure 6.3. How do these data change or support the questions or hypotheses you just generated?

The Wagon Wheel can also be used for purposes other than evaluating student learning data. Since anything that can be defined can be measured, and anything that can be measured can be placed on the Wagon Wheel, let's take a look at how you can use the Wagon Wheel to evaluate teacher performance using the most recent Interstate New Teacher Assessment and Support Consortium (InTASC) standards update as a definition of excellent teaching for the purpose of measuring excellence. Originally developed in 1992, the 2010 version of InTASC was developed by a consortium of educators representing every major education organization in the country, including teacher associations and college preparation programs. The new standards are designed to be compatible with the range of national teacher and leader standards currently in use as well as the recently released common core for students in math and language arts. The goal of InTASC is to develop a common set of standards for preparing, licensing, and evaluating teachers across the country. The consortium is seeking to begin a national conversation to explore how these standards can be used to improve the quality of teaching including building a bridge to National Board Certification, which we know has a direct impact on improving student achievement outcomes. For more information, visit *www.nbpts.org*.

■ USING THE WAGON WHEEL TO MEASURE InTASC STANDARDS

The Wagon Wheel can be used by teachers to plot their progress toward competence in each standard as a reflective exercise. As opposed to using these standards to measure others, what if teachers reviewed the performance indicators for each standard and then collected evidence (videos, work samples, photographs, sample lessons, student achievement data, reflection, and surveys) to demonstrate their progress on each standard? Not only would such a process be more meaningful than an outside assessment but staff members could visually see with the Wagon Wheel where they were and where they needed to be on each standard. If building principals conducted this activity with all staff members, they would get great data about which standard (or standards) the teachers need additional training to master. The ability to improve with targeted feedback, training, and support is the cornerstone to improving the quality of teachers. The ten InTASC standards are organized into four domains: learner and learning, content knowledge, instructional practice, and professional responsibility.

Figure 6.3 Writing Example: Fourth Grade, 2009–2011

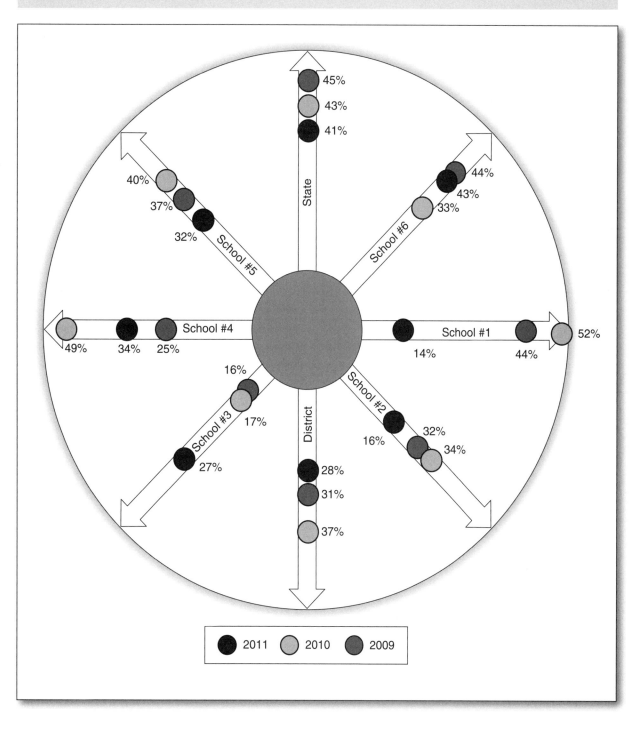

What do you notice about these data? What additional questions do you have?

Learner and Learning

This domain focuses on three standards: learner development, learning differences, and learning environments. The main focus of this collection of standards is the learner (students) and the teacher's relationship to the learner. Effective teachers not only understand where each learner is in his or her development but they also understand the differences between each learner and seek to differentiate instruction to meet those needs. They provide high-quality and challenging work to meet the needs of each learner. They also work with the learners to create a classroom environment that is positive and supportive of each student. Each of the InTASC standards has a sentence that describes the standard and performance targets for teachers that fall into three categories: performances, essential knowledge, and critical dispositions. The number of performance targets varies according to the standard but within a range between 10 and 20 for each one. The specificity in these performance targets allows districts, preparation programs, and licensing agencies a wide variety of applications in using the standards to define excellence in teaching.

Content Knowledge

Included in the content knowledge domain are the standards of content knowledge and innovative applications of content. Content knowledge includes using tools of inquiry that can make the content relevant and meaningful to the learners. The standard of innovation applications in this domain focuses on a teacher's ability to connect concepts. The standard of knowledge focuses on a teacher's ability to not only understand the central concepts of his or her content but also to understand differing perspectives within the content to engage learners in creative thinking and creative problem solving related to real world local and global issues. Whereas the first domain focuses on a teacher's relationships with learners, this domain emphasizes her or his ability to make content relevant to learners.

Instructional Practice

The three standards associated with this domain are assessment, planning for instruction, and instructional strategies. The focus of the assessment standard is on the teacher's ability to understand and use multiple methods of assessment in order to engage learners in their own growth, document their learning progress, and guide ongoing planning and instruction. Using assessment as a way to intrinsically motivate students is the focus of this standard. Planning for instruction looks at the teacher's ability to draw upon knowledge of content, skills, the learners, the community, and pedagogy to plan instruction that supports all students in meeting rigorous learning goals. Instructional strategies focus on teachers being able to use a variety of strategies to encourage learners to develop a deep understanding of the content and apply that content in a variety of settings. This domain can be summed up in one word: rigor. Through assessment, planning, and effective strategies, teachers can provide rigorous instruction for their students that helps them reach their full potential as learners.

Professional Responsibility

The final domain of professional responsibility addresses the need for educators to practice reflection and continuous growth in their practice and how that practice affects other people (students, families, colleagues, and community). The final standard of the ten is collaboration. Effective teachers collaborate with students, families, colleagues, and others to share responsibility for student growth, learning, and well-being.

The InTASC standards are a great addition to the national conversation about improving teacher quality, but if they only sit on a shelf, they will not make a difference for students in the classroom. It is no mystery that the practice of coaching and support improves performance more than grading and judgment. If teachers used these new standards as a way to benchmark growth, achievement, and progress toward excellence in teaching, their progress and reflection could be tracked and visually reported to others on a Wagon Wheel.

IN THE FIELD: USING THE WAGON WHEEL TO ANALYZE RTI EFFECTIVENESS

A district team wanted to track several different data points to see if there was any correlation between the effective implementation of Response to Intervention (RTI) and the percentage of teachers with master's degrees, years of experience, schoolwide test scores, attendance, and poverty rates (see Figure 6.4). RTI is a system of prevention and intervention that the federal government wrote into its reauthorization of the Individuals with Disabilities Education Act (IDEA) in 2001. RTI encourages and allows districts to use IDEA funds (up to 15%) to provide intervention for students who have not yet been identified with a disability for the explicit purpose of providing timely support and possibly preventing a disability. Through RTI, the federal government created a means for specialists to work with unidentified struggling students to avoid a disability label later in their schooling.

Prior to this rule change, it was not allowable for students without disabilities to be instructed by disability specialists without the burden and expense of months of testing. This approach also encourages more rapid intervention. The results for districts implementing RTI have been very encouraging. Instead of suspecting a disability and following up that suspicion with months of assessment, schools, through their data teams, can identify students who are struggling and attempt interventions with experts to see if the interventions make a difference. Students who do not respond to intervention efforts may, in fact, have a disability. At this point, these students would be able to qualify for additional services. RTI helps schools be efficient with their resources and responsive to student needs.

In Figure 6.4, four different schools were chosen, all with similar socioeconomic status (SES) demographics (between 80% and 90% of their students qualified for free and reduced lunch). There are a variety of school-based assessments that can help determine how well a school has implemented RTI. This district team wanted to see if a school's score on its RTI assessment correlated with other data. An analysis of the Wagon Wheel (Figure 6.4) shows a correlation between a school's reading test scores and its RTI implementation. Further study will reveal which comes first—a solid RTI implementation or improved reading test scores. The district's hypothesis was that test scores would go up as schools learn how to implement RTI effectively. Initial results led data teams in that direction, but additional study and analysis over the course of multiple years is needed to solidify that conclusion.

Figure 6.4   RTI Effectiveness

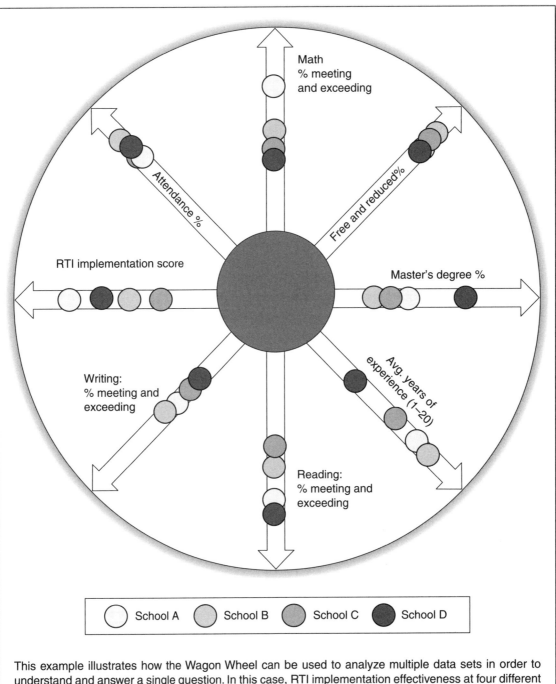

This example illustrates how the Wagon Wheel can be used to analyze multiple data sets in order to understand and answer a single question. In this case, RTI implementation effectiveness at four different schools is correlated to other data in an effort to discover possible patterns and to help understand the context and conditions that will help RTI be implemented effectively.

PUTTING IT ALL TOGETHER ■

The power of synthesis can never be underestimated. The Wagon Wheel is a synthesis tool that empowers data teams, individuals, and schools with the ability to process multiple data points in a quick amount of time to facilitate the solving of complex problems. School and district improvement and reform are not easy work. It requires wrestling with tough issues and digging beneath the surface to get at the root of stubborn problems and issues. The Wagon Wheel helps data teams move from the paralysis of a tough problem to analysis in order to make a difference.

Martin Luther King, Jr. was the ultimate Wagon Wheel. He listened to and synthesized data from individuals. He mobilized large groups of people to move together in a cohesive fashion to accomplish a remarkable goal. He fought for the rights and freedoms of people in this country, and though the struggle was ferocious, he was successful in his quest. In the 21st century, educators are fighting for the economic rights of their students and the opportunity to make the world a better place. By continuing to improve outcomes for students in our public schools through the use of the Wagon Wheel, educators can confidently answer Dr. King's question, What are you doing for others?

7

Five Whys

The Power of Questions

*Not everything that can be counted counts, and
not everything that counts can be counted.*

—Albert Einstein

Author, blogger, and social commentator Seth Godin lists the following reasons why people work (Godin, 2010c):

1. For the money

2. To be challenged

3. For the pleasure/calling of doing the work

4. For the impact it makes on the world

5. For the reputation you build in the community

6. To solve interesting problems

7. To be part of a group and to experience the mission

8. To be appreciated

Godin goes on to pose this hard question, "Since most people keep going to work each day because of reasons two through eight, why is so much emphasis placed on reason one?" In the best-selling book, *Drive*, Daniel Pink (2010) answers that question by explaining through extensive research that money is a relatively shallow, extrinsic motivator. Its importance lies in helping people feel they are getting a fair wage for their work. If people are not getting paid fairly, it is hard for them to advance to Levels 2 through 8. However, once a fair wage is earned, it is reasons two through eight that pave the way to doing great work, and great work leads to great results.

■ TOOL 7: FIVE WHYS

The tools in this book support problem solving and higher level thinking. They help individuals and teams move beyond the extrinsic force of reason one and into the intrinsic reasons of two through eight. They assist members of data teams in looking thoughtfully at their data and making strategic decisions in team settings that make a difference. The result is quality learning experiences that culminate in student achievement.

The Five Whys tool is the first tool in this book that is primarily qualitative as opposed to quantitative. Five Whys is a systems-thinking tool that helps teachers, administrators, and even students think outside the box for solutions and identify actions that have a powerful impact on results. This qualitative tool helps educators explore the relationship between causes and effects, and it helps identify strategies to explore the complex and persistent problems that face us every day. Instead of looking at numbers to make sense of where students are, data team members explore potential causes of results with the goal of solving a persistent problem by determining what to do next.

Five Whys was popularized by Toyota engineers who were trained to ask five *why* questions for every problem they encountered. The discipline of asking *why* questions forced the engineers to make connections beyond their own division or department in order to solve complex problems. Asking *why* questions breaks down silos and mobilizes teams to act in a unified direction when it comes to wrestling with persistent problems and looking for solutions. Why questions force us to think and look deeper to solve systemic problems.

Persistent Achievement Gaps

Figure 7.1 illustrates a Five Whys activity that was conducted in a school district that has high and low socioeconomic status (SES) schools with predictable, long-standing achievement gaps. With relatively few exceptions, the schools from high-poverty neighborhoods consistently performed worse on standardized tests than their more affluent neighbors. The process of exploring this persistent problem began with the *why* question, Why does an achievement gap exist between high and low SES schools? Staff members reflected on the question and wrote down all of the possible reasons for the problem. Then they shared their reasons, and a facilitator placed the reasons into categories based on similarity. The major causes that surfaced through the process were as follows:

- Silos (staff working in isolation) exist between high and low SES schools and district services.
- Quality programs do not exist in all schools.
- Intense historical poverty creates additional barriers to success.
- There are gaps in early literacy and social capital (experiences and opportunities) between students from poverty and their middle-class peers.
- It is perceived that the most effective teachers generally gravitate away from high-poverty schools.

Figure 7.1 Five Whys: Closing Achievement Gaps

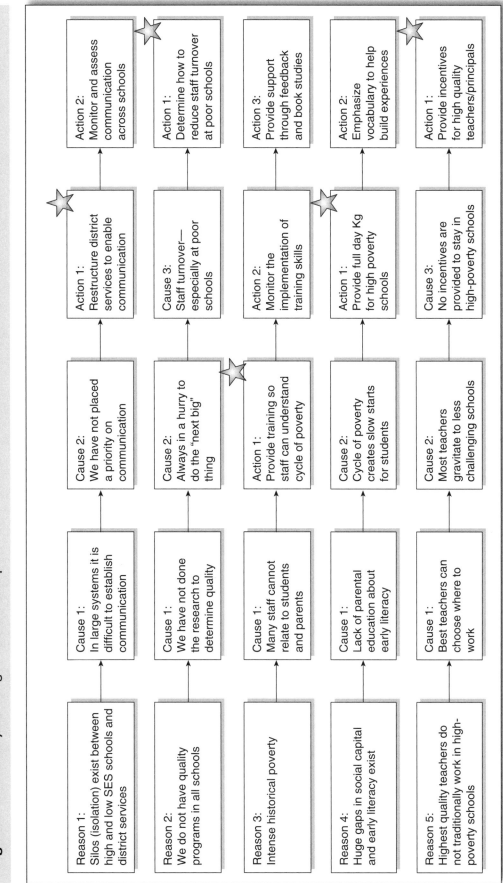

Reason 1:
Silos (isolation) exist between high and low SES schools and district services

Cause 1:
In large systems it is difficult to establish communication

Cause 2:
We have not placed a priority on communication

Action 1:
Restructure district services to enable communication

Action 2:
Monitor and assess communication across schools

Reason 2:
We do not have quality programs in all schools

Cause 1:
We have not done the research to determine quality

Cause 2:
Always in a hurry to do the "next big" thing

Cause 3:
Staff turnover—especially at poor schools

Action 1:
Determine how to reduce staff turnover at poor schools

Reason 3:
Intense historical poverty

Cause 1:
Many staff cannot relate to students and parents

Action 1:
Provide training so staff can understand cycle of poverty

Action 2:
Monitor the implementation of training skills

Action 3:
Provide support through feedback and book studies

Reason 4:
Huge gaps in social capital and early literacy exist

Cause 1:
Lack of parental education about early literacy

Cause 2:
Cycle of poverty creates slow starts for students

Action 1:
Provide full day Kg for high poverty schools

Action 2:
Emphasize vocabulary to help build experiences

Reason 5:
Highest quality teachers do not traditionally work in high-poverty schools

Cause 1:
Best teachers can choose where to work

Cause 2:
Most teachers gravitate to less challenging schools

Cause 3:
No incentives are provided to stay in high-poverty schools

Action 1:
Provide incentives for high quality teachers/principals

Once possible reasons are determined, staff explored each one by asking a series of *why* questions with the expressed purpose of drilling down to the root causes in order to discover an action or actions that could be taken to address the problem. As you can see from Figure 7.1, each of the bulleted reasons listed previously were addressed with the following specific actions the district could take to narrow and ultimately eliminate the achievement gap:

- Restructure district services to increase frequency and effectiveness of communication between high and low SES schools so that best practices can be shared across sites.
- Reduce staff turnover (teachers and principals) at high-poverty schools by creating a positive, learning-focused collaborative culture.
- Provide training for staff members in high-poverty schools so that they can understand the cycle of poverty and be better equipped to work and connect with students and their families in meaningful ways.
- Provide full-day kindergarten, along with enhanced vocabulary instruction and literacy experiences for high-poverty schools where achievement gaps exist.
- Work with union partners to develop meaningful incentives that encourage high-performing principals and teachers to continue working at high-poverty schools.

The advantage of working through a Five Why activity is that all stakeholders are at the table working and thinking together about complex problems so that the solutions generated have greater ownership as well as support. The process of thinking through what to do is a valuable component in moving to action. School improvement work is difficult and requires strong support to empower teams to work through implementation and its challenges. Implementation of actions to solve persistent problems requires significant resources in terms of time, attention, effort, and sometimes money. Using a School Improvement Map (Chapter 10) after you have determined which actions to take through a Five Why activity can be an extremely helpful next step in the improvement process as well.

A Diverse District Beating the Odds

Montgomery County Public Schools (MCPS) in Maryland is arguably one of the most diverse school districts in the country and one of the largest in the country, with over 125,000 students. MCPS has proven that achievement gaps can be closed and the bar raised for all students, even in some very poor and diverse neighborhoods. The district's story is chronicled in the book *Leading for Equity* (Childress, Doyle, & Thomas, 2009). Its success hinged on a stage of change framework that contains five components:

1. Innovate and monitor: Understanding the importance of innovating to determine what works, followed by strong implementation and monitoring of best practices.

2. Align systems and structures: Making sure that promising practices are discovered and best practices are scaled throughout the district. Moving from hero leadership to systems that ensure ongoing success.

3. Identifying existing conditions: Constantly looking at data to determine where the needs are and deciding what is working and not working.

4. Establish meaningful expectations: Expectations drive success for everyone—staff, students, parents, and community stakeholders.

5. React: Trying to limit reacting to fads, fashions, and new initiatives. Keeping the main thing, the main thing takes tremendous discipline.

Whereas most school districts spend the majority of their time at Number 5, reacting to the latest whims of legislation, the board, state department, or powerful unions, MCPS staff members spent most of their time at levels one and two discovering best practices and scaling those practices by designing and implementing effective systems. They discovered the power of benchmarking their success to seven college readiness skills that were designed by working with teachers and administrators *(www.montgomeryschoolsmd.org)*. The Montgomery County story is proof that given the right kind of training, support, professional development, and focus, urban districts can close gaps and raise achievement.

Schools Beating the Odds

Even though they are not the norm, it is not difficult to find schools that have closed achievement gaps across the country. Books such as *It's Being Done* (Chenoweth, 2007), *No Excuses* (Lopez, 2009), and *Teach Like a Champion* (Lemov, 2010) are being written and published on a regular basis. Nearly every state in the union has some way to identify schools that are beating the odds so that other schools can visit and learn how they did it. Invariably these success stories reveal that there are no shortcuts. There is no silver bullet. Every school is unique, but gap closers do have some things in common. Without a doubt, you find in these schools rampant internal motivation and an insatiable drive to meet student needs by all stakeholders—teaching staff, classified staff, parents, and the community. Random acts of leadership regularly occur in a supportive and collaborative environment.

As Daniel Pink (2010) confirms in his research on the subject, once people feel like they are being paid a fair wage for their work, cash incentives do little and might even do harm for people engaged in complex, difficult tasks that require new ways of thinking and working to improve. Leadership, on the other hand, is something that should be encouraged throughout every level of the organization, and the concept of paying people for additional duties and responsibilities that support leadership is a performance pay model that makes sense. Incentives should reinforce the behavior we want to see more of, and in education, we need more teamwork and collaboration—not competition.

The Power of Working Together

The recent emphasis on professional learning communities (PLCs) has demonstrated the importance of analyzing data in teams. PLC work falls into four categories: data work, standards work, intervention work, and student work.

Teachers must have regular time built into their schedules to look at student achievement data in teams. They have to be able to work together analyzing standards, developing learning targets, and designing assessments that measure progress toward those learning targets. In teams, they need to design and implement interventions in response to their formative data while targeting improvement summative data. And yet, all of this is not enough. Teachers need to spend time looking at actual student work. They need to observe students in learning settings and reflect upon what they see.

Phil Schlechty (2002) reflects, "Good school work is engaging school work, but not all engaging school work is good work" (p. xviii). The work that teachers design for students must be meaningful, challenging, and stimulate thinking. The design of student learning experiences is ideally accomplished in teams where the synergy of ideas is released in such a way that students ultimately prosper.

Because teamwork is so important, schools may wish to measure the level of teamwork and collegiality occurring at their school. One of the most effective long-standing tools is the culture survey developed by Penelope and Corps (1990). With this simple 17-question survey, leaders can assess their schools in the three important areas of professional collaboration, collegial relationships, and efficacy.

■ TEACHING STUDENTS TO THINK

When Dr. Suess died in 1991, the world lost a prophet. Even in the early 1990s before we had the technology to declare a teacher effective or less effective based upon how students performed on standardized tests, he saw the writing on the wall and explained it for the rest of us in *Diffendoofer Day*, the last book he ever wrote. The setting is a small school in danger of being closed that needs good test scores to stay open. The book opens with a description of all the wonderful teachers and staff at Diffendoofer School who are teaching their students amazing things about the world in which they live. Unfortunately, the school is under pressure to perform on a standardized test and will be shut down if it doesn't do well on the exam. The principal, Mr. Lowe, is very worried, but Mrs. Bonkers (the heroic teacher) tells him not to fret because, in her words, "We've taught them that the Earth is round; that red and white make pink; and something else that matters more—we've taught them *how to think*" (Suess, Prelutsky, & Smith, 1998, p. 26) Needless to say, the school is saved when the students ace the test.

In *The Global Achievement Gap*, Tony Wagner (2010) stresses the importance of teaching students to think and how few of today's classrooms (even in some of our better schools as judged by test scores) are actually teaching students to think. Wagner documents learning walks through 20 classrooms in three high-achieving schools. The study revealed only one classroom was actually preparing students to think at high levels and consistently preparing students for college. The 21st-century workplace is one that requires thinkers, learners, leaders, and creative problem solvers.

In the best-selling book *Linchpin,* author Seth Godin (2010a) discusses the workplace of tomorrow and the importance of developing linchpins—people that matter and are indispensable employees. These workers are not easily replaced. They do more than what is asked of them. They take initiative. They solve problems. They are leaders. They think creatively. Godin (2010a) argues that schools should really only teach two things: how to solve interesting problems and how to lead. Those will be extremely marketable skills deep into the 21st century.

21st-Century Skills: The Future Is Now

EdLeader21 (*www.edleader21.com*) is the nation's first professional learning community dedicated to supporting school districts that are committed to teaching students the four cornerstone standards of the 21st century: critical thinking, communication, collaboration, and creativity. Headed by Ken Kay, there are currently over 30 districts across the country participating in this network. This organization understands the importance of thinking, creativity, exploration, and discovery as the reform strategies of the future. The staff members are committed to supporting 21st-century skill implementation and are flying in the face of the status quo, based on testing, teaching to the test, and establishing rewards and punishments based on test results.

IN THE FIELD: IMPLEMENTING A CORE PROGRAM

When it comes to school improvement efforts, a lack of fidelity in implementing core reading and math curriculum is a common complaint from administrators and teacher leaders. Figure 7.2 illustrates how the Five Why tool can uncover actions a team can take to improve the implementation of a core curriculum effort. In this example, the team surfaced the following reasons for the lack of implementation:

- Teachers don't see a value in the curriculum.
- Schools and teachers have too much autonomy when it comes to curriculum implementation.
- Core curriculum is not effective.

Using the Five Whys tool, each reason was explored by asking a series of *why* questions. When the team members were asked why the teachers didn't see a value in the curriculum, they responded that the teachers were minimally involved in the development process. When asked why they were not involved, the group deduced it was due to a lack of organization. Why did the lack of organization exist? Because it was not a priority of the implementers of the program to get teachers and principals involved.

The team decided it was time to get teachers involved, and it decided the best way to do that was by providing training for teachers and principals in the curriculum. In this case, teachers currently using the curriculum helped deliver the training. One of the most important action steps this activity identified was the need for principals to be trained in the importance of a common purpose when it comes to curriculum adoption.

Figure 7.2 Five Whys: Implementing Core Curriculum

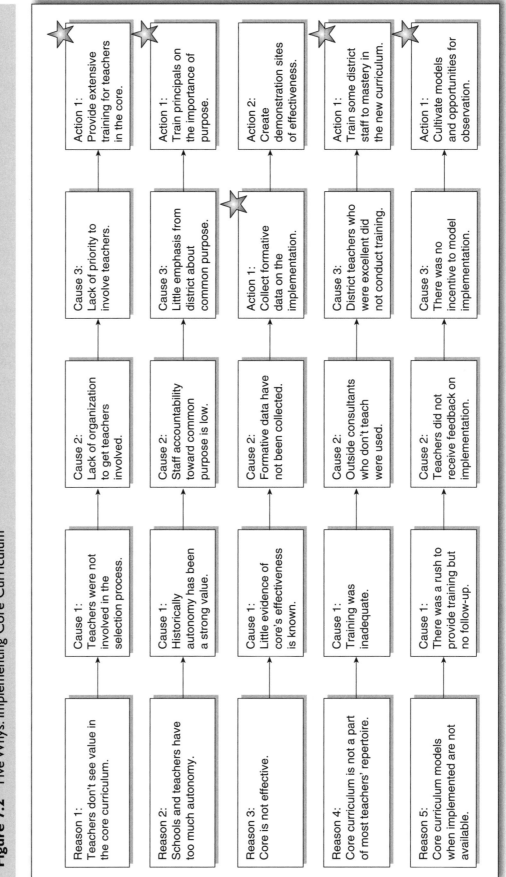

PUTTING IT ALL TOGETHER ■

In *Drive,* Daniel Pink (2010) emphasizes that intrinsic motivation is the difference maker between people who just show up to work and those who are constantly learning and growing toward excellence. The best thing you can do to help a school improve is to lead staff members toward being intrinsically motivated by the work they do.

According to Pink (2010), people must have the elements of purpose, autonomy, and mastery to migrate from survival (Motivation 1.0), to extrinsic *carrots and sticks* (Motivation 2.0), to intrinsic excellence (Motivation 3.0). Only Motivation 3.0 is dedicated to continuous improvement. It takes that kind of commitment from teachers and principals to see sustainable school improvement that eliminates gaps and raise achievement for all.

In Pink's model, the purpose of the organization or activity must be clearly understood. Autonomy only becomes a powerful lever when the purpose is clear to all. If principals do not understand the purpose and value behind a new curriculum, there is little hope that teachers will be able to move toward mastery in the material. Autonomy is only a powerful force when it is linked to purpose and directed toward mastery.

As we move forward in the 21st century, we will discover that schools that close gaps, outperform expectations given their demographics, achieve breakthrough results, and help students reach their full potential are the ones that put meeting the needs of students first—above everything else—and galvanize the power of their stakeholders to institutionalize the capacity to serve students in quality ways. The research is clear. Organizations that strive to serve rather than conquer are gaining market share and outperform their peers (Sisodia, Wolfe, & Sheth, 2007). It is really through selfless service to others that we learn, grow, and improve. This is a profound reality in the world of education. It is only through the selfless service to others that we begin to help students reach their full potential.

Schools and districts built on serving students first and striving to serve other stakeholders (parents, community, and staff) second close gaps, raise achievement, and create citizens that dream, explore, and discover as leaders, thinkers, and learners in the 21st century.

8

Relations Diagram

Discovering the Key Drivers

*Leadership involves getting others to willingly move in a
direction they're not naturally inclined to move on their own.*

—Harry Truman

Which came first, the chicken or the egg? The roots of this ageless debate
can be traced to the Greek historian, Mestius Plutarchus who in 90 AD
wrote an essay titled *Table Talk* (Thims, 2008). The essay debates the origin of life
itself. Well, in the summer of 2010, scientists at Sheffield and Warwick
Universities in England discovered the answer (Freeman, 2010). It turns out the
egg cannot be formed without the protein ovocledidin-17. This protein is the
essential ingredient that allows the shell to develop and it is produced solely
inside the ovaries of the chicken. Therefore, their research concluded, the egg
must be produced inside the chicken. The chicken came first.

Makes sense, doesn't it? It also helps to have a hen to incubate an egg so that
it will hatch, but even with science weighing in on the side of the chicken, this
question will most likely still be debated but not for a lack of evidence. This
chapter illustrates how using the Relations Diagram can facilitate identifying
the driving cause behind tough questions or problems using all available data
so that better decisions can be made and improved outcomes occur.

TOOL 8: RELATIONS DIAGRAM ■

When staff members, teams, districts, or nations are faced with entrenched,
complex, and persistent problems, the Relations Diagram can be used to determine the key drivers of a particular problem so that interventions can be targeted, strategic, and effective. This tool requires staff members to identify the

problem to be solved and to agree on that problem. Once agreement is reached, all possible causes are brainstormed and presented in a circle around the problem. From there, each cause is individually analyzed to determine its impact on other causes.

The process for completing a Relations Diagram can take 90 to 180 minutes. Teams emerge from this activity with a problem they agree on, an understanding of the driving causes of that problem, and unified strategies for attacking the problem. In this way, the right problem is solved as opposed to a more superficial one that might result if careful analysis was not part of the process. This tool is best used in smaller groups or teams. It can also be used with students to explore the causes of the Civil War or other complex issues. Since it often stimulates a great deal of debate and problem solving, it is less effective in a whole-group staff meeting. If it is used in the staff meeting context, small table groups can complete the Relations Diagram process and each table group can share their results for the purpose of comparing and contrasting responses.

Tackling Discipline Problems

A high school had a reputation for students exhibiting poor behavior. Teachers complained of losing valuable instructional time because of the discipline problems. Principal after principal came and left. Each one tried a variety of strategies to fix the problems, but nothing seemed to work. Staff members felt stuck. They had several years' worth of data demonstrating that attendance was poor and inappropriate behavior was a common occurrence. But the presence of data wasn't enough to solve the problem. In many ways, the data were debilitating because they were a constant reminder of the problem, but never led to a solution. Data alone never do. Data can indicate there *is* a problem. It is only by working with the data (via reflection and various tools) that problems can be identified, key drivers can be identified, and strategies selected to address those problems.

Using the Relations Diagram is a vibrant approach to addressing a specific problem. It is particularly useful when a team has discouraging data that it has wrestled with unsuccessfully for a period of time without strategic decisions regarding a course of action. The Relations Diagram is a tool that helps participants explore possible causes for entrenched problems and work together to identify which cause is a key driver of the other causes. In this way, data teams can identify strategies to address the key drivers and work to focus on the key items that are impacting and influencing others. Since energy becomes concentrated, powerful results can be achieved.

The high school staff members used the Relations Diagram (see Tool 8 on page 130 for a blank version to photocopy) to identify the driving force behind their history of student behavior problems by identifying all of the tangible problems or causes. Some problems are more visible than others and therefore easily identified. Other problems take some time to uncover.

During the problem identification phase of the Relations Diagram, participants identify potential problems on sticky notes, one note per problem. This reflection portion of the process can take 15 to 20 minutes. Provide participants plenty of time to think about what is going on and write down the problems as they perceive them. A group of five to seven people may come up with over 20 problems.

After the reflection time, collect the problems and put them in categories. Have team members do the work of clustering by similarity and label the categories as they emerge. In the example of the high school with severe student behavior problems, there were over 20 problems, but all of those problems fell into the following categories:

- The students in the school historically have had poor behavior.
- Behavior expectations are not posted.
- There are different expectations in every classroom.
- There is a lack of accountability for teachers to follow the rules.
- There is a lack of training for new staff members.
- The office staff members do not communicate expectations and roles to teachers.
- There is a lack of information and training for staff members on common school rules and policies.
- Teachers do not communicate roles and responsibilities to students.

Notice that poor parenting or a lack of community supports did not surface as a problem. This is not because those things didn't exist, but they didn't surface as problems during the exercise and that is what makes the Relations Diagram so powerful. The people closest to the work are the ones who define the problem, propose solutions, implement those solutions, and measure the impact of implementing their solution strategies. Tapping into the people closest to the work is the best way to improve systems.

This was the secret to the Montgomery County Public Schools (MCPS) turnaround (Childress, Doyle, & Thomas, 2009), and why the Creative Leadership Achieves Success (CLASS) grant sponsored by the Chalkboard Project *(www .chalkboardproject.org)* has been so successful in the Northwest. CLASS is a collaborative leadership project that brings administrators and teachers together to design evaluation systems, professional development, leadership opportunities, and compensation models. These joint projects have been launched in school districts throughout Oregon and have resulted in several creative models that make sense and support excellence in the classroom (Castillo, 2011)

After the problems are agreed upon and identified, it is time to see how they relate to each other. The goal of this step in the process is to determine which of these problems is driving or causing other problems. Each of the identified problems in our high school example was placed in a circle on a large white board (Figure 8.1).

After the problems are identified, they are examined individually and rated against the other problems by asking this question of the group, Which problem drives or causes the other problem? For instance, in the example above, did the fact that students have historically behaved poorly cause behavior expectations not to be posted, or did the lack of having expectations posted cause historic behavior problems? By weighing each cause against the other causes, team

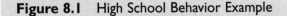

Figure 8.1 High School Behavior Example

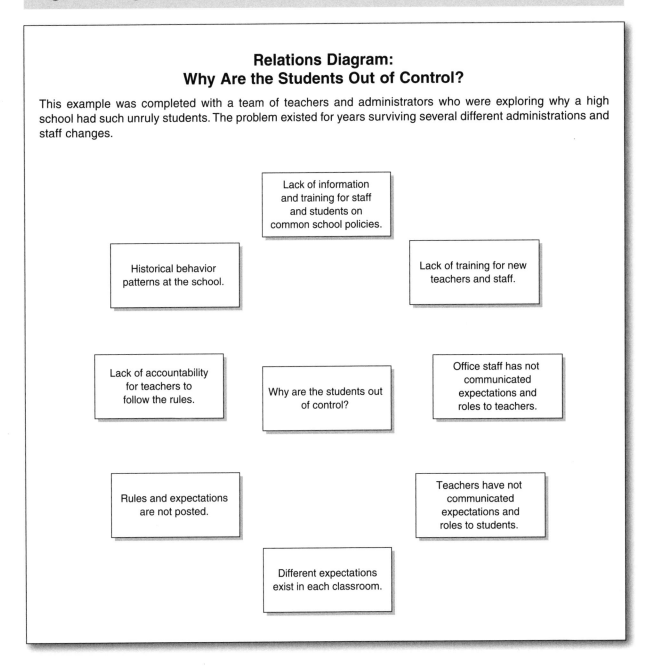

Relations Diagram:
Why Are the Students Out of Control?

This example was completed with a team of teachers and administrators who were exploring why a high school had such unruly students. The problem existed for years surviving several different administrations and staff changes.

Lack of information and training for staff and students on common school policies.

Historical behavior patterns at the school.

Lack of training for new teachers and staff.

Lack of accountability for teachers to follow the rules.

Why are the students out of control?

Office staff has not communicated expectations and roles to teachers.

Rules and expectations are not posted.

Teachers have not communicated expectations and roles to students.

Different expectations exist in each classroom.

members discuss, debate, and decide which problems drove or caused the other ones. In the rare case when consensus cannot be reached between problems and their impact on others, team members vote to determine the key driver.

When the process is complete (see Figure 8.2), the key drivers emerge, and the team positions itself to focus strategies toward taking actions that have the greatest influence. Using this process, the high school team identified two key drivers: (1) a lack of training and information on common rules and policies and (2) policies and office staff not communicating expectations and roles to teachers. Finding a few key drivers from over 20 initial problems is typical. After the process, staff members were energized to take strategic, data-driven actions that had a greater chance of making a difference.

Figure 8.2 High School Behavior Problem Key Driver Example

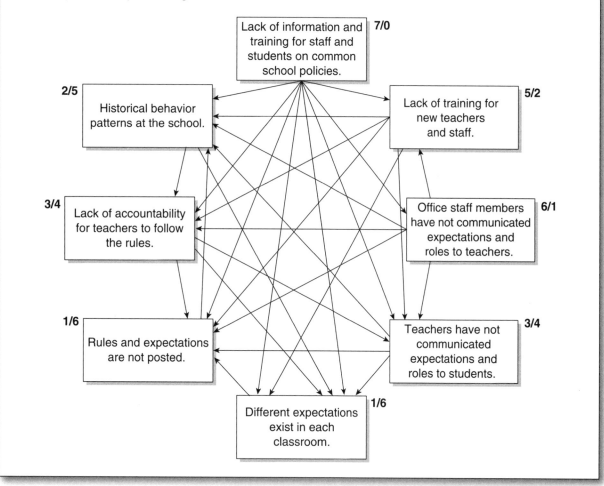

Relations Diagram: Determining the Key Drivers

To use the Relations Diagram, the team looks at each cause and determines which causes are the strongest drivers. Each cause is measured against other causes individually. One by one around the diagram, the team decides which cause drives the other causes. The stronger cause is depicted with the arrow pointing away from the cause. As you can see in this example, "lack of information and training for staff members and students on common school policies" is the number one driver (7/0) followed by "office staff members have not communicated expectations and roles to teachers" (6/1). Using this tool helps teams know what action they need to take to solve the problem they are facing.

The most remarkable thing about the Relations Diagram is that through this process staff members often embrace solutions and strategies that they previously resisted. Notice the two key drivers that were identified in this example: a lack of training for staff and a lack of reinforcement from the office. Through this process, the team agreed it needed training and that administration should reinforce and support that training, holding staff members accountable for taking part in the training and implementing strategies. How often does that happen when leaders roll out *the next new thing*? Rarely. But because staff members were at the center of solving the problem, they embraced the solution. The next new thing is replaced with a new way doing business—continuous improvement. The Relations Diagram generates a deep commitment to getting better together.

Motivating Students

Recently the Relations Diagram was used to design motivation strategies for middle school students at a K through 8 school. Anyone who teaches or works with middle school students knows that motivation with this group is always a factor when it comes to doing school. The middle school psyche can love, hate, and love you again all in the space of one class period. The middle school teachers at this school were eager to prevent another spring fallout in terms of losing the battle of student motivation. Staff members voiced the need to create the conditions that would motivate students in early January during their weekly faculty collaboration time.

With the aid of the Relations Diagram, staff members identified the following drivers as contributing factors to the apparent lack of student motivation:

- Lack of parental involvement and support
- Lack of accountability for not completing work
- Lack of positive role models
- Lack of academic skills
- A norm of social promotion
- Lack of meaningful incentives
- Quality and type of work provided to students

In this case, the team members determined through the Relations Diagram that a lack of parent involvement and support was the key driver to low student motivation, but when it came to implementing a strategy, they wanted to focus on something they had more control over. They realized they could create a consistent accountability system across their classes and could have complete control over the implementation of that intervention. By implementing a simple system of requiring students to do uncompleted school work during their lunch recess, they immediately got additional effort from students during the time they should be working on assignments in class.

They found a reasonable "stick" that meant something and used it in a logical way. The message was a clear one: "If you waste instructional time during class by not working, you lose some of your free time. We care more about you completing your work than we care about our own lunch. This work matters." This strategy had an immediate impact for most of the students. There were still some yellow and red zone students who needed additional interventions, but by consistently applying that single strategy, they increased student motivation to complete the assigned work.

Another key driver teachers perceived they had significant control over was the opportunity to expose the students to other adults who were successful in life and have these adults share their stories about the importance of education and completing schoolwork. Students often hear from their teachers again and again about the importance of school and learning, but how often do students get to hear from other adults about the importance of education, especially if they come from homes where the adults did not have positive educational experiences or encounter success at school? Even in those homes where both parents have college degrees, many students have built up immunity to the supportive words about the value of education from their parents and teachers.

Successful adults who benefited from education were able to speak to this group of students about their achievements and the importance of trying one's best in school. As a result of this effort, students wrote letters of thanks to the many adults who took the time to speak with them. It made a difference.

Transforming student motivation for middle school students in the 21st century is not a one-and-done event. It is demanding work that requires a variety of ongoing, learning-focused strategies and consistency over time, but this is a problem that can be addressed and resolved by using the Relations Diagram. A dedicated team of educators willing to examine their instructional practices and what they can control, and then have the tenacity to follow through on what they propose to implement, will see improvement in the problem they target. What a team pays attention to and communicates becomes what is valued.

The final action this group of teachers took was to restructure how they organized their teaching schedules in order to increase the relevance of and expertise in their content area. Relevance has big payoffs in terms of student motivation, and they wanted to see the impact of restructuring their curriculum and content. Since this was a major undertaking, they did the planning necessary to make the change in the spring and then implemented the new structure in the fall.

In this new schedule, teachers got the opportunity to focus in their content area of strength (to increase relevancy) and created movement for students during the day to increase variety, rigor, and relationship with significant adults. Their commitment to being willing to do whatever it takes to see improvement in student motivation drove this group of teachers to change their practices. The new structure they implemented allowed for more teaming opportunities and the ability to create more engaging and meaningful work for their students—work that required their students to think, solve interesting problems, and learn to lead. Together, these collective efforts paved the way to enhanced learning experiences for their students that resulted in increased student motivation. These professionals paved the way to a better learning experience for their students.

IN THE FIELD: READ 180 REVISITED

A teacher leader in a large middle school was wondering why the number of students placed in an expensive, research-based reading intervention program, READ 180, was only 50% of the capacity of the program. The school's data on statewide assessments revealed the need for interventions was much greater. Given those data, all of the slots should be filled. The teacher leader and school administration speculated that the reason the program was only at 50% capacity was because teachers didn't understand it, nor were they aware of the referral process for getting students enrolled.

Rather than send more e-mails and memos explaining the referral process and urging teachers to use it, the teacher leader gathered together the language arts teachers and used the Relations Diagram to dig deeper into the reasons why the program

(Continued)

(Continued)

was underutilized and identified what they could do together to address the problem. The team initially listed 41 causes for the problem. They eventually came up with the following categories:

- Absenteeism
- Loss of elective time when participating
- Scheduling problems
- Lack of teacher awareness/understanding of how READ 180 works
- Perception of classroom teacher responsibility to support struggling readers as opposed to sending them to an intervention by a specialist
- Lack of data collected to determine who needs the intervention
- Lack of available classroom screening tool

Through the Relations Diagram activity, it was determined that teacher awareness, education, and understanding of the program were the key drivers of the other problems. The teacher leader took his findings to administration leaders, and they designed plans to do something about the lack of teacher awareness. They arranged for every teacher to spend some time working in the READ 180 lab to understand the program and see the activities in which students were engaged. Through this process, the teachers became advocates of the program and worked through the other major driving forces. Ultimately, the Relations Diagram helped staff members learn more about and use a vital resource to foster student learning.

■ PUTTING IT ALL TOGETHER

The most remarkable thing about the Relations Diagram is that within the space of one, 3-hour session, a room full of disengaged, unmotivated, problem finders transforms into a room of highly motivated troubleshooters committed to doing something differently. The key to making things better through continuous improvement is rooted in a simple willingness to change. Movement or momentum in a data-driven situation helps team members feel they are making progress. The specific steps ground team members in a concrete process that yields specific, immediate results.

Movement matters when it comes to persistent problems that no one knows how to fix—because that's why the problems persist. A motionless ship can't be steered, but once moving it has a chance. Rudder work is easy when you have wind. Harry Truman would appreciate the Relations Diagram. It is a great tool for getting a team moving in the direction you want it to go. So, the next time a data team is deep in a chicken and egg debate, use the Relations Diagram to direct your next strategic move!

9

The Fishbone

Making a Difference With Data

*Every breakthrough we have experienced has been
the result of a break with how we used to do things.*

—Stephen Covey (2004)

In 1997, Apple computer was on the brink of disappearing, and it very well may have disappeared if Microsoft had not invested $150 million dollars in the fledging company (Abell, 2009). Flash forward 13 years to May 2010 when Apple surpassed all other technology companies in market share, including Microsoft and Google. The Apple comeback is truly one of the most remarkable business turnaround stories our generation has witnessed. How did it happen and what changed in 1997 besides the return of CEO Steve Jobs? In a fast-paced complex world with a short attention span, how much of a difference can one person really make?

LEADERSHIP MATTERS ■

The leaders that really make a difference, "power of one" leaders, are driven to make things better and to work with those around them to do that very thing. If they are in public education, they work with their boards and unions. If they are in government, they work with their constituents. They keep the vision first and foremost and refuse to compromise. They are driven by an unwavering quest for improvement. They improve a meeting by simply walking into the room. Steve Jobs was driven by the vision of simply making products that work, and everything that Apple does still puts improving the customer's experience at the front of the line. With such an attitude, it is no surprise that Apple won the technology wars.

Real Education Reform

Gaston Caperton, a two-time governor of West Virginia from1989 to 1997, has been making a difference in education for over twenty years. In 1989, Caperton inherited a government on the brink of bankruptcy with more than $500 million in debt. By the time he completed his terms, the state had a surplus of $100 million. He created 86,000 new jobs causing unemployment to drop from 9.8% to 6.2%. Education was his number one priority. His fiscal approach to improving the economy of West Virginia led *Financial World* to call West Virginia "the most improved state in the nation (College Board, n.d.)

In support of education, Caperton initiated an aggressive school construction program that invested $800 million into building and renovating schools across the state. The program directly benefited two thirds of the children in the state. He also developed a comprehensive plan called the West Virginia Basic Skills Computer Program that emphasized the use of computers and technology in kindergarten through sixth grade and later expanded the program to include grades seven through 12. He trained over 19,000 West Virginia educators through a center for professional development with a goal of putting technology to its best use throughout the state. In 1996, these advances in technology grew national attention when he received the Computerworld Smithsonian Award. Caperton was recognized as having fundamentally changed the use of technology in education in America. In 1997, Education Week conducted a study of the nation's education system and held out West Virginia as the leader in using technology in education (College Board, n.d.)

Gaston Caperton's ability to make a difference in education didn't stop with being the governor of West Virginia in 1997. He became the president of the College Board in 1999. The College Board, developer of the SAT test, has been around since 1900. Under Caperton's leadership, it has become much more than a testing organization. In many ways, an argument can be made that Caperton has in his quiet and supportive way transformed high school education in America through the Advanced Placement (AP) program.

Caperton believes the experience of higher level thinking opportunities that students experience in AP coursework can change their lives. When he took the helm of the College Board in 1999, only about 3% of high school students in America participated in AP coursework. In 10 short years, that number has exploded to over 20%. In some of the top high schools around the country, students graduate having taken more than 10 AP courses in their high school career. Caperton's vision that all students can benefit from challenging coursework and high standards is taking hold and changing how teachers teach and students learn.

Fueled by Caperton's philosophy, the College Board launched teacher training programs for AP coursework, and participation among minority students and students of poverty in AP courses dramatically increased. The exams and coursework for the AP program is consistent around the country—one of the few examples of a national curriculum that means something beyond high school. Schools that want to offer AP courses and teachers who want to teach them must submit their syllabus to a national organization for an external review process. The process maintains the rigor of the course-work even as more and more schools offer the curriculum.

Like many districts across the country, Montgomery County Public Schools (MCPS) staff members used the AP program to benchmark their high school reform efforts. Over the last decade they significantly increased access to AP coursework, the number of AP tests given, and passing student scores on AP tests. Participation among minority students outpaced all other subgroups. They also discovered that students who took at least one AP course during their high school career had a six-year college success rate double that of students who did not participate in the program (Childress, Doyle, & Thomas, 2009).

The rigor of the SAT test has increased during Caperton's tenure as well by adding a writing component, advanced mathematics, and replacing reading anthologies with critical reading passages. Under his leadership, *www.college board.com* was launched, providing clear planning and preparation routes for students, parents, teachers, and administrators that help over 4 million students prepare and plan for college each year. It is by far the most user-friendly and accessible website for college and career planning. In the 21st century, college ready equals career ready, and the College Board has taken that mantle seriously by providing advice, support, and access to all.

What the College Board has done to transform the rigor of high school through a national network of support and service is far superior to what a host of educational organizations, institutions, policymakers, and foundations have been trying to achieve during the same time period—take No Child Left Behind (NCLB) as a case in point. Many today call it a failed policy that simply needs to be discarded (Ravitch, 2011). In an age where results matter, the College Board, headed by Gaston Caperton is a difference maker for good.

Making a Difference in the Classroom

To fully grasp the difference one teacher can make, consider what Los Angeles Unified educator Rafe Esquith has achieved in his fifth-grade classroom. Documented in his books, *There Are No Shortcuts* (2004) and *Teach Like Your Hair's on Fire* (2007), Esquith has run the ultimate demonstration classroom for over 20 years. Students in his fifth-grade classroom read real books, solve interesting problems, produce a play by Shakespeare every year, have daily physical education (PE), and learn to play guitar at lunch time. Yes, Rafe works hard. He routinely opens his classroom for students at 6:00 a.m. and works with students until 6:00 p.m. Rafe's students do remarkably well in his classroom. Many of them arrive two to three years behind grade level (as measured by standardized tests) and leave above grade level. All of his students come from high-poverty, minority backgrounds. All of his students qualify for free and reduced lunch and not a single one comes from a family that owns its home, yet during the course of a year with Mr. Esquith, these students become scholars. He inspires them to go to college. He has been making magic happen in Room 56 of Hobarth Elementary School for over 20 years, and he has the data to prove that many of his students do go to college—even ivy league colleges—and they excel once they get there.

In spite of all his classroom success, Rafe's greatest contribution may be how he influenced other educators—two of whom launched a movement based upon his classroom instruction. Michael Fienberg and David Levin were so inspired after seeing a presentation by Rafe, they wondered if his "no shortcut" method of longer hours and more rigorous (higher level thinking) approach to teaching and learning could be scaled from one classroom to an entire school. In 1994, they discovered it could, and when their high-poverty elementary school got local attention with some remarkable results, people with money began to notice. Knowledge Is Power Program (KIPP) schools were born, and as of the fall of 2011, the movement had 99 schools in 20 states systemically closing achievement gaps in high-poverty, high-minority, urban and rural communities. Proving yet again, that with powerful instruction, exceptional systems, and parental support just about anything can be accomplished in a school. Every movement starts with an idea, and ideas start with individuals.

TurnAround Schools *(www.turnaroundschools.com)* is another example of how a few committed people have made a remarkable difference. TurnAround Consulting sponsors a network of schools taking college readiness to a whole new level by supporting No Excuses Universities across the county. Educators at No Excuses Universities believe they have the power to influence every student to be academically successful—even those who are most at risk. Founded by brothers Damen and Dan Lopez, the No Excuses University revolution is sweeping the country. At the time of this writing, there are over 100 elementary and middle schools that have joined the No Excuses network.

As a result of joining the network, learning best practices together, and a laserlike focus on effective instruction, the learning and achievement results in these schools is greatly improving. Learning gains come from staff members getting involved in the work of aligning their instruction, assessing that instruction, analyzing the data that come from that assessment, and implementing interventions that make a difference. The Lopez brothers currently serve over 56,000 students within their network of schools. Their Big Hairy Audacious Goal (BHAG) is to serve 1 million children across the country. Knowing Dan and Damen and the power of their model, we have no doubt they will get there—it is just a matter of when.

The fact that small groups of people can make such a remarkable difference should thrill us. Why do these people matter so much? Because they are driven to make life better for others. They didn't sign up for personal gain or attention, and they are not looking to leave a legacy. They just want to make a dent in the universe, and they surround themselves with great people, build exceptional teams, and simply do what is right by keeping the needs of children first and foremost. Sustainable reform must move beyond talented individuals and islands of excellence to teams that make a difference—and that's where the Fishbone can help.

■ TOOL 9: THE FISHBONE

The power of the Fishbone lies in helping teams make a difference by exploring the causes behind positive results or investigating results that are less than what was hoped for in order to make the necessary changes so that improvement can occur. In the Fishbone examples that follow, we examine the causes of low tenth-grade math scores (see Figure 9.1), what it took for a seventh-grade classroom to achieve a 100% passing rate on the state writing test (see Figure 9.2), and how an elementary school achieved breakthrough results in math and reading (see Figure 9.3).

Improving Tenth-Grade Math Scores

Figure 9.1 reflects the thinking of what a math department went through when it made a commitment to improve tenth-grade math achievement. Having experienced multiple years of flat to declining math scores, the Fishbone was used to illustrate the process of improvement.

Step 1: Brainstorm the Question

The team listed all of the reasons why the students were not being successful on the Fishbone. Team members wrote the reasons why they believed the scores were low on sticky notes. The facilitator of the meeting gathered the notes and with the assistance of the team placed those reasons into categories. As you can see from the example of Figure 9.1, there was a wide range of reasons for the poor performance. Some of those reasons will be beyond the team's control and some will not be. The key to the exercise is capturing what the team is thinking in a visual way.

Step 2: Analyze the Reasons

The analysis can occur in a variety of ways. Individuals can rank the reasons on a scale of 1 to 10 according to which reasons are the biggest drivers, and then the group can discuss what each person is thinking. They can be analyzed in terms of what the team can and can't control, or any other way that seems appropriate. In the example of Figure 9.1 the reasons are not ranked. For an activity in this book, data team members can write down the reasons they think were the biggest drivers.

Step 3: Reflect and Respond

In this step, the team reflects and decides what it wants to do next. Through this process, the team decides what interventions need to occur, what needs to stop, and what current practices need to be improved. Through this process the team working on improving math scores decided to develop common assessments, change the school schedule so students had math every day, and invest in a new problem solving based curriculum.

Everyone Writes

Figure 9.2 is an example of how the Fishbone tool was used to examine how every seventh grader passed the state writing test in one classroom when the average percentage of students passing the test statewide is below 50%. Data on this

Figure 9.1 Math Improvement Needed

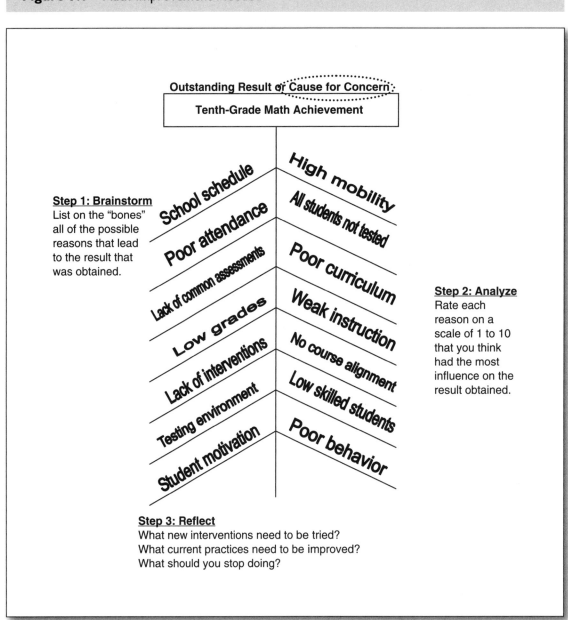

Fishbone also include some key strategies schools have used over time to improve writing. Take a moment to reflect on all of the reasons and speculate which ones had greatest impact in this seventh-grade classroom's rise to excellence.

According to the students who achieved this result, the number-one reason they excelled was because they wrote in every subject, every day. Using reflective journals, they spent a great deal of time doing all kinds of writing. Another key leverage point for the class was learning how to write a five-paragraph essay. The teacher spent time teaching the students this structure, which is similar to four-square writing, where students take a piece of paper and fold it into four squares. In the middle of the paper, they write their main idea, and

Figure 9.2 Effective Writing Program: Seventh Grade

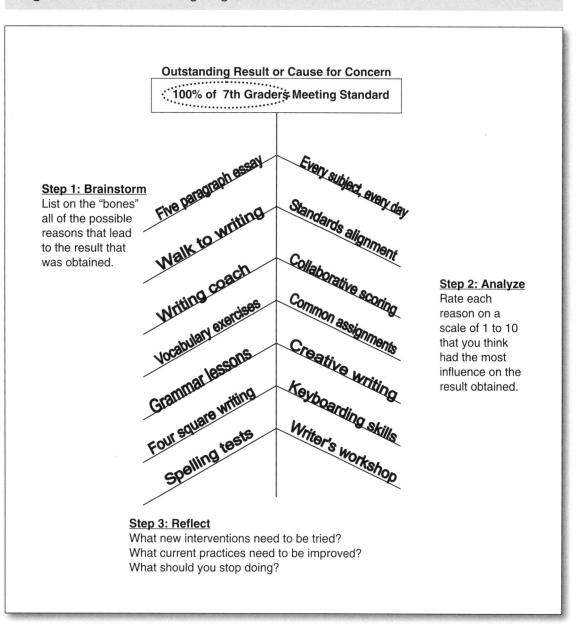

then they write three supporting details in three of the boxes, followed by a summary sentence in the fourth box. The method is extremely structured, but it teaches students to think about any subject in a logical way and to effectively organize their thoughts.

It is interesting to note that these students did not become great at writing from grammar lessons or spelling tests. They achieved excellence because they did authentic writing on a regular basis and shared that writing with each other. Schools seeking to improve writing need to have students write every day, collaboratively score that writing, and use writing as a vehicle to deeply understand whatever content is being presented.

IN THE FIELD: GREEN ACRES, THE PLACE TO BE

Green Acres was not always the place to be. Over the past 20 years, the community surrounding this neighborhood school slowly changed. As new neighborhoods were developed in town, many stable families left the area. As a result of this population shift, the percentage of students in Green Acres who qualified for the free and reduced lunch program in Green Acres rose to over 85%. Along with the poverty status, the school also has the highest minority population, English language learners, special education students, and mobility of any school in the district. However, when the state assessment results were released for the 2009 to 2010 school year, Green Acres boasted the highest gains of any school in the district and nearly outperformed them all as well. How did the school do it? A fishbone was used to find out (see Figure 9.3).

Staff members discussed several causes that contributed to the breakthrough results. Included in this list was a school schedule that enabled teachers to collaborate up to an hour every day while the students rotated through lunch, recess, and enrichment activities supervised by classified staff. This unique schedule, a brainchild of the former principal, allows for daily discussions among staff members where grade-level teams collaborate around student data, curriculum, and make decisions regarding how to intervene with struggling students.

Staff members also stressed the importance of creating a testing environment that provided students with the opportunity to do their best work and identified the fact that retaining key teachers in math was critical to their success. Staff members spent a year increasing their cultural competence in working with students from poverty backgrounds through Donna Beagle's (2007) poverty framework. This framework helped staff members understand the culture their students were coming from and allowed them opportunities to meet student needs in deeper ways so that barriers between staff and student thinking could be bridged.

Instructionally, the teachers organized around content area specializations by grade level. Some teachers specialized in language arts and social studies while others became experts in math and science. Teachers shared cohorts of students, and the fewer areas of preparation allowed each teacher an opportunity to develop deep expertise in his or her content areas. As a result, the lessons teachers delivered were highly engaging, consistently beyond the textbook, and involved authentic reading, writing, thinking, and speaking opportunities. The school was the first to acquire and experiment with a problem-solving-based math curriculum. In addition to curriculum that required deep thinking, all of the support staff members consistently reinforced the instruction that occurred in the classroom as opposed to pulling students out of core reading and math instruction to deliver an alternative core of some kind. Second and third doses of instruction were aligned to what was happening during regular instruction.

However, innovative best practices aside, staff members felt there was one element more powerful than any other that led to their breakthrough result—a sense of community. The Green Acres staff described a sense of togetherness and support that transcended formative and summative assessments. At Green Acres, every student is supported by the staff. Students don't fall through the cracks, because a web of support and a can-do approach permeates all that is said and done.

Figure 9.3 Reading and Math Score Increase

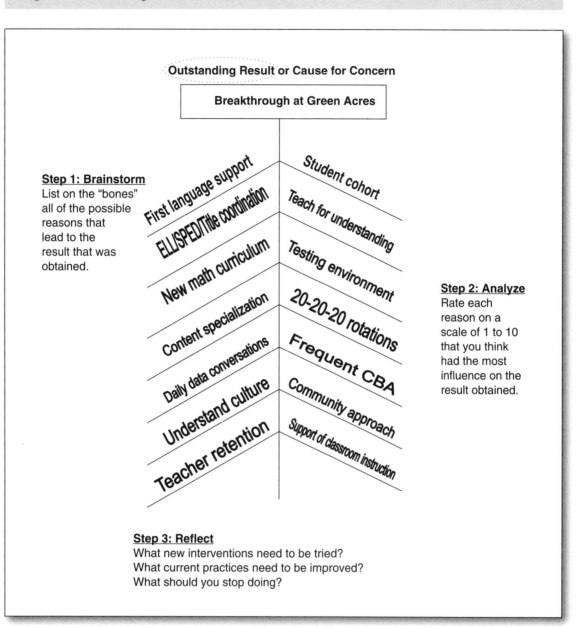

PUTTING IT ALL TOGETHER ■

School, district, and national education reform must focus on building exceptional systems as opposed to finding really talented superstars. In his article, "The Myth of Talent" Malcolm Gladwell (2002) writes convincingly that we have overestimated the importance of talent. Citing the fall of Enron as the example of how not to build a business, Gladwell makes the case that smart, impressive superstars end up being more concerned with self than service.

The me-first attitude eventually gets them in trouble because these stars are not team players, and in the 21st century, everyone is required to play and work in teams to be successful. Teaching is no longer an individual sport. The data tools in this book can all be used to enhance teamwork and cooperation. Organizations that win and schools that close achievement gaps know and understand the importance of working in teams to achieve remarkable results. When schools develop remarkable systems, they begin to understand the power behind systems. Effective systems (as opposed to individual teachers or principals) make every individual better, and as a result, the team becomes better than the sum of its parts.

The reform of public education will not occur without the development of exceptional systems. Whether it is Apple, TurnAround Consulting, KIPP, Montgomery Public Schools, or the College Board, exceptional systems have been built by these organizations, they are being built in other places around the country, and they are making a difference. It is our humble hope that the tools in the toolkit will help you to make a difference in your professional learning community work as you seek to make a difference for students in your corner of the world.

10

School Improvement Mapping

Making Strategic Decisions and Taking Action

Activity—to produce real results—must be organized and executed meticulously. Otherwise, it's no different from children running around the playground at recess.

—John Wooden, UCLA basketball
coach from 1948 to 1975

Planet Earth lost an icon in the summer of 2010. John Wooden, legendary basketball coach for the UCLA Bruins during the 1960s and 1970s, died at the age of 99. Wooden dominated his sport during his generation. In his last 12 years of coaching at UCLA, he won 10 national championships, had four perfect seasons, and at one point during this stretch, his teams won 88 straight games! No college basketball coach has even come close to achieving these feats. Even though he is arguably the best coach in any decade in any sport, few people realize that Wooden coached for 28 years before he won a national championship. Achieving excellence takes time and commitment. There are no shortcuts.

John Wooden, however, didn't consider himself a coach. He considered himself a teacher first, and the gym was his classroom. An English major in college, he loved literature, especially Shakespeare, and he never would have gone into coaching at all if a graduate fellowship that allowed him to pursue a professorship had paid enough money to support his young family (Wooden & Jamison, 2005).

In the debates about great coaches, John Wooden's name is always on the short list. And yet, in spite of dominating his sport for over a decade, Coach Wooden never talked about winning. He never gave speeches to his team about winning, not even before it took the court for national championship games. He was consumed with one thing: improvement, the art of constantly getting better, and he had a system for doing just that.

As a teacher, Wooden incorporated the best elements of great teaching into his basketball practices. He was compulsive about controlling what he could control, and that obsession caused him to script out his practices minute-by-minute, incorporating a variety of drills that constantly increased the skills of his players. He understood the foundational principle of improvement that we so often forget when it comes to pursuing better outcomes—don't focus on results. Get better at what you do every day, and once those building blocks of success are in place, the results will follow.

■ TOOL 10: SCHOOL IMPROVEMENT MAPPING

School Improvement Mapping (SIM) is a qualitative tool used for sketching out improvements over time. Professional development is an important element of SIM. SIMs focus teams on what they *will do* to improve their work as opposed to what they should or could do if they had more time, resources, better people, leaders, and so on. SIMs move teams from strategic planning to strategic actions. A well-executed SIM will generate actions to be taken quickly and to engage the team in a positive direction. Typically, the SIM is used after the team has identified an improvement goal.

A SIM is used to script out the moves or actions that will make the most difference to achieve a school improvement goal. Once the map has been sketched, the team can refer to it as it executes the plan. The map can serve as a motivator and guide to daily, weekly, and monthly activity. In this way, changes in practice can be tracked over time, achievements can be celebrated, and more people will become engaged with the demanding and difficult work of implementing plans for school improvement. SIM has three main components: goal setting, strategies, and activities.

Goal Setting

SIM begins with goal setting. Every school improvement plan requires some sort of goal-setting process. Meaningful goals must have the support and buy-in of those who are doing the work of school improvement. Many times, goals are written as a required act of compliance. Goals that get accomplished—goals that matter—must have the emotional and intellectual support of those who are working on them. In their breakthrough book on change, Dan and Chip Heath (2010) document the importance of connecting a goal to the emotional and/or intellectual part of the brain and the difference it makes to do so, in keeping that goal in the forefront of stakeholders' minds. It is better to have one meaningful goal than pages of goals that no one values or remembers. Using data to illustrate a need is one of the most effective ways to get people intellectually on board with goals. Notice the goal in the SIM sample (see Figure 10.1). It is specific and measurable.

Figure 10.1 School Improvement Destination (Goal): Increase the Percentage of Students Proficient in Writing From 43% to 75%

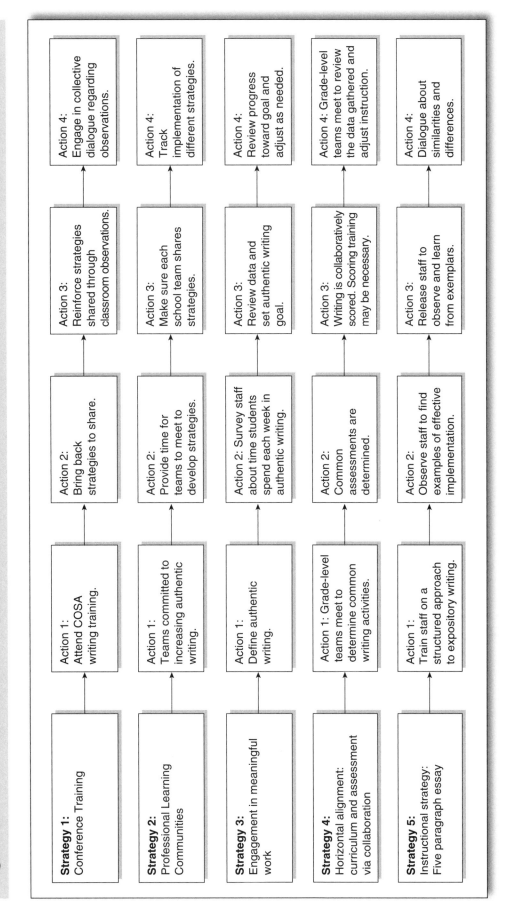

Strategy 1:
Conference Training

Action 1:
Attend COSA writing training.

Action 2:
Bring back strategies to share.

Action 3:
Reinforce strategies shared through classroom observations.

Action 4:
Engage in collective dialogue regarding observations.

Strategy 2:
Professional Learning Communities

Action 1:
Teams committed to increasing authentic writing.

Action 2:
Provide time for teams to meet to develop strategies.

Action 3:
Make sure each school team shares strategies.

Action 4:
Track implementation of different strategies.

Strategy 3:
Engagement in meaningful work

Action 1:
Define authentic writing.

Action 2: Survey staff about time students spend each week in authentic writing.

Action 3:
Review data and set authentic writing goal.

Action 4:
Review progress toward goal and adjust as needed.

Strategy 4:
Horizontal alignment: curriculum and assessment via collaboration

Action 1: Grade-level teams meet to determine common writing activities.

Action 2:
Common assessments are determined.

Action 3:
Writing is collaboratively scored. Scoring training may be necessary.

Action 4: Grade-level teams meet to review the data gathered and adjust instruction.

Strategy 5:
Instructional strategy: Five paragraph essay

Action 1:
Train staff on a structured approach to expository writing.

Action 2:
Observe staff to find examples of effective implementation.

Action 3:
Release staff to observe and learn from exemplars.

Action 4:
Dialogue about similarities and differences.

Using Data to Drive Goals

In the fall of 2010, the five-year trend in writing scores in a school district looked like this:

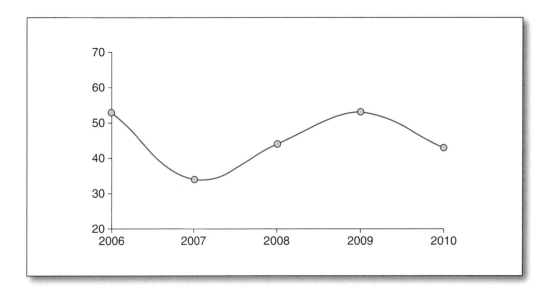

The fact that less than one half of the students were proficient in writing and that the percentage had actually declined in the last five years was shocking to most staff. The visual graph of a roller coaster ride had an emotional impact as well. Clearly, there was not a consistent focus on writing across the district. It wasn't hard for school staff members to take this data and map out improvement strategies that would focus on improving student writing in their buildings.

Goals must also be measurable. In other words, they should declare a destination so a team knows when it gets there or are getting close. Goals should also stretch the limits of what the team thinks is possible. Goals that don't get people's attention don't get their focus, and without focus, nothing gets accomplished. In the classic book *Good to Great*, Jim Collins (2001) writes about what he calls A Big Hairy Audacious Goal (BHAG). What he discovered in his research is that organizations that set BHAGs tend to get a lot more accomplished than ones that simply try to make incremental moves. The incremental growth plan tends to be boring. It doesn't grab people's attention, doesn't stir up motivation, and is easy to forget. The whole purpose of SIM is to get people to engage and do things that will change the status quo and influence all organizational members in ways that help them grow.

Clear Strategies

Clear strategies are the next major component of SIM. Training is an important element of any map, but it's in the strategy section where the type of professional development to be provided is explained. Delineating strategies with clarity helps organizational members know what is being worked on so that they can focus on the strategy.

When implementing strategies, context is king. Every school and setting is different. What worked in one school or district may not work in another. Schools are not static. They are dynamic. School cultures, leadership, and classroom instruction are three variables that differ widely across schools and can promote or deter improvement efforts. When selecting strategies for school improvement efforts, it is essential to consider contextual variables.

Specific Actions

Actions give legs to strategies. Through effective actions, data teams put energy and effort in place so that schools can move beyond the status quo. Clear action steps create a pathway to determine whether specific strategies will make a difference in school improvement. When completing a SIM, each strategy needs three to five action steps to help the school move toward its declared destination. Action steps are the key behind all improvement work. Nothing gets improved without them. They must be clear, and the team that develops them is responsible for making sure they get implemented, monitored, and assessed.

Improving Writing Districtwide With Goals, Strategies, and Actions

In the quest to prepare more students for college and careers, the ability for students to write effectively surfaces as a critical skill. There is no substitute for it. Writing is thinking on paper, and in nearly every college course, students will be asked to write. Their ability to write effectively will be vital to their ability to communicate successfully in college, career, or life. Figure 10.1 shows an example of how a district or school can script out an improvement plan that focuses on student writing.

You will notice that there are only five strategies listed to achieve the stretch goal of having writing improve from 43% proficiency across the district to 75% proficiency across the district. Obviously, there may be more than five strategies necessary to achieve this goal. In the example, there are four actions or activities listed for teams to achieve each strategy. Naturally, when you are attempting to move to the next level in your results, you may need additional strategies. Do not worry about the number. The intent is to have clear destinations (goals), several explicit strategies, and as many action steps as necessary to get the team moving beyond the status quo. With this approach, there are no limits to what a committed team of people can achieve.

CREATING THE BUILDING ■
BLOCKS OF EXCELLENCE

At the time of this writing, the book *Teach Like a Champion* (2010) by Doug Lemov is currently one of the best-selling books in education. Why? The book is incredibly practical. It contains 49 different skills that all teachers who want to improve can use in their classrooms to increase student engagement and learning. The book contains strategies like *No Opt Out* that instructs teachers to go back to the student who answers a question with "I don't know" and have the student repeat the right answer. *Teach Like a Champion* reads like a John Wooden basketball practice for teachers. If you practice the skills, you will become highly effective. Focused skill building improves the instructional effectiveness of the individual teacher and consequently, the classroom. But what are the major ingredients that will impact the entire system? The three building blocks for school and district improvement are hiring, professional development, and evaluation.

Hiring the Best

Todd Whittaker (2003) states that the quickest way to improve your school is to hire quality people. He believes the key principle to organizational improvement is "you are who you hire." The hiring process should never be rushed. Hiring and marriage are the only two times you get to pick a family member, and mistakes are painful. The hiring process should be deliberate and include several steps: extensive reference checking, interview questions that reflect what someone has done as opposed to what he or she thinks, demonstrations of proficiency, and input from multiple people. Jeff Bezos, founder and CEO of Amazon.com once said he would rather interview 50 people and not hire any of them than hire the wrong person (Carmichael, n.d.). School improvement starts from within, provided you have great people working within. Hiring the best available talent accelerates the improvement process.

Great companies know this to be true. Documented in the books *Topgrading* (Smart, 2005) and *Who* (Smart & Street, 2008), the Smart father and son duo demonstrate again and again how the best companies in America use detailed and extensive strategies to recruit and hire the best available talent for their key positions. They share those strategies with the rest of us in their books. In a school district, every teacher and principal is a key position because each one's impact has such a long reach.

Finding quality staff members and hiring them is not as easy as it seems. In most states, it takes an extra year or two of formal education beyond a bachelor's degree for an individual to get a teaching license. Malcolm Gladwell, author of *Outliers, Blink,* and *Tipping Point,* wrote an article for the *New Yorker* in which he compared being able to hire a good teacher to being able to find an NFL quarterback from the ranks of college football (Gladwell, 2008). His point? The college game is so much different from the pro game that it is virtually impossible to predict beyond an accuracy of 30% to 40% who will become a great professional quarterback and who will not based upon the body of an athelete's work in college. Often, the same is true for teachers. Teaching involves a rapid stream of context-based decisions and corresponding behaviors. Teaching quality is difficult to assess in practice until an individual is in a classroom, interacting with students, and the outcomes of these interactions can be examined over time.

According to research done by Eric Hanushek at Stanford University, students who have the good fortune of being in a classroom with a great teacher will average up to a year and one half of academic gains in reading and math (Gladwell, 2008). Students languishing in the classrooms of poor-to-average teachers will average about one half of a year's growth. The stakes are extremely high to find the best teachers possible, hire them, and provide the support they need to reach their highest potential. Teacher development must begin with practical preservice preparation.

Professional Development

Edward Deming (1986), one of the founders of the modern continuous improvement model, considered training to be the cornerstone of any organization trying to get better. Training is essential. In education, it is only through effective professional development that we demonstrate we value employees as learners and unleash the opportunity for each person to reach his or her full potential as leaders and facilitators of learning. Providing ongoing professional development and support not only communicates that we value teachers and other school leaders as professionals but that we consider the work they are doing as vital, ever changing, and challenging. As a consequence, there is a continual need to reinvent oneself and grow professionally. Professional development that results in school improvement should include

- presentations of new ideas,
- opportunities to work in teams based on topics of choice,
- opportunities to work with teams to ensure that curriculum and assessments are rigorous and aligned horizontally and vertically between grade levels,
- job-embedded training around specific skills,
- the use of data to make informed decisions,
- availability of demonstration classrooms, and
- exceptional mentor programs that are differentiated according to need.

Though exceptional hiring is the quickest way to improve a school or district, powerful, results-orientated professional development is the only way to make sure that the school and district are continuously learning and improving.

Evaluation for Meaningful Feedback

Many people have negative feelings about evaluation. Others embrace it wholeheartedly. What is the first thing that comes to mind when you hear, *evaluation*? Is it fear or an opportunity to learn and grow? Feedback from meaningful evaluation is a critical ingredient for school improvement. Fullan, Crévola, and Hill (2006) write that the quality of classroom instruction is "the most important condition for successful school reform" (p. 28). The quality of classroom instruction has been shown to be the largest leverage point for fostering student learning. Effective evaluation enhances teaching skillfulness in the classroom.

Improving Instructional Feedback

The University of Virginia's Curry School of Education has meticulously researched the effective practices of teachers in the classroom by reviewing hundreds of hours of videotaped classroom instruction (Gladwell, 2008). The educators discovered that feedback—direct, personal response by a teacher to a specific statement by a student—is the most important factor in helping improve student learning and achievement. It is our belief that the same holds true for helping teachers improve. They need meaningful feedback and support to get better.

In the book, *Instructional Rounds,* the authors argue that task predicts performance, and if schools want to see gains in student learning and achievement, they need to focus on the tasks that students are doing in the classroom, and those tasks need to be high-quality ones that make students think (City, Elmore, Fiarman, & Teitel, 2009). Focusing on the tasks teachers provide to their students and helping them continually develop higher quality tasks is the most effective way of improving achievement outcomes.

In Mike Schmoker's (2011) most recent book, *Focus,* he explains the centrality of authentic literacy (reading, writing, and discussion) to unlocking all content areas and laments the fact that in the majority of classrooms today, students do not have enough time to practice those essential skills and get meaningful feedback upon their performance. He documents as well that in-the-moment meaningful, formative feedback (checking for understanding) is the most important element for helping people learn.

We need to adjust our thinking when it comes to evaluation and change the dialogue. We need to realize that learners benefit most from meaningful feedback, and if we have the courage to provide formative and summative feedback in ways that maintain dignity and respect, improved classroom performance will be a natural occurrence. A focus on improving the process of instruction through data teams and peer feedback will yield better results than focusing on the actual results. Meaningful feedback is the goal, and we need to look at evaluation as such. Teacher evaluation systems should not be the end of the game. High-stakes decisions, based upon data provided after the whistle has blown and everyone has gone home, should happen in the moment with meaningful feedback so that teachers can get better at their craft and learning can improve.

■ THE POWER OF MENTORING AS AN IMPROVEMENT TOOL

Dr. Ben Carson is a brilliant brain surgeon. In his book, *Think Big: Unleashing Your Potential for Excellence,* Dr. Carson (2006) tells the story of how he moved from the academic bottom of his fifth-grade classroom in poverty-stricken Detroit to become head of neurosurgery at The Johns Hopkins University, one of the best teaching hospitals in the country. He describes the mentoring support he received along the way from four different public school teachers who helped make his journey possible. Dr. Carson's story is not unique.

Several research studies and firsthand experiences written by Donna Beagle (2007) demonstrate that one of the most effective strategies to help students break the poverty barrier is adult mentoring. Mentoring can take on many forms, from coaching to clubs and counseling to classrooms. Students who break through the poverty barrier and become the first person to attend college in their family usually do so through a support system of multiple mentors. It takes more than academic know-how and skill to make it to college. In addition to the academic skills of reading, writing, and math that must be mastered, there are webs of inside information about what it takes to succeed in college that must be learned as well. SIMs can reflect the importance of mentoring as an intervention strategy.

Author and education reformer David Conley (2010) articulates just what it takes to succeed in college in his latest book, *College and Career Ready*. Dr. Conley not only documents the academic skills necessary for college and career readiness but also discusses the skills of learning how to study, manage time, and ask for help among other things, because it is not just getting to college that is important; it is knowing how to persist and finish what you started once you arrive. In 2008, the six-year college completion rate in the United States was only 55%,—and that number has barely moved in the last decade (NCHEMS Information Center, n.d.).

One of the most exciting mentoring projects happening in America right now is a grass roots effort launched from Portland, Oregon. Inspired by Donald Miller, author of *Blue Like Jazz* (2003) and *Father Fiction* (2011), the Mentoring Project *(www.thementoringproject.org)* is seeking to change the lives of 1,000 fatherless children by connecting them with adult mentors. Through the project, volunteer mentors are matched with young people and provided with training and resources so that they can have the maximum impact upon the young people.

School improvement teams can also map out what it takes to implement a mentoring program. Mentoring programs can and should be implemented at every school, and they will look differently depending on the school level being targeted. Some of the strategies to include in a mentoring program are identification of the target population of students, training for mentors (adult and student), parent notification and support, data analysis of mentees, and activities for involvement. Figure 10.2 includes an example of a mentor program that can be implemented at the high school level, but the same principles could be applied at a middle or elementary school.

Moving to the Next Level: A New Model of Systemic Improvement

SIM is the heart of the bigger task of systemic improvement. Systemic improvement is about getting an organization to the next level by moving through the seven steps illustrated in Figure 10.3.

SIM is designed to take students to higher levels of success. Moving to the next level is like climbing a staircase. There are seven steps between each platform. Before we start scaling those stairs, it is important to understand the absolute necessity of collaboration, which is the railing that holds all of the steps together. Collaboration is more important today than it has ever been before. In the 21st-century workplace, and in professional learning communities (PLCs), small teams play a vital role in promoting productivity.

Figure 10.2 School Improvement Destination (Goal): Increase the Number of Mentors and the Effectiveness of the Mentor Program

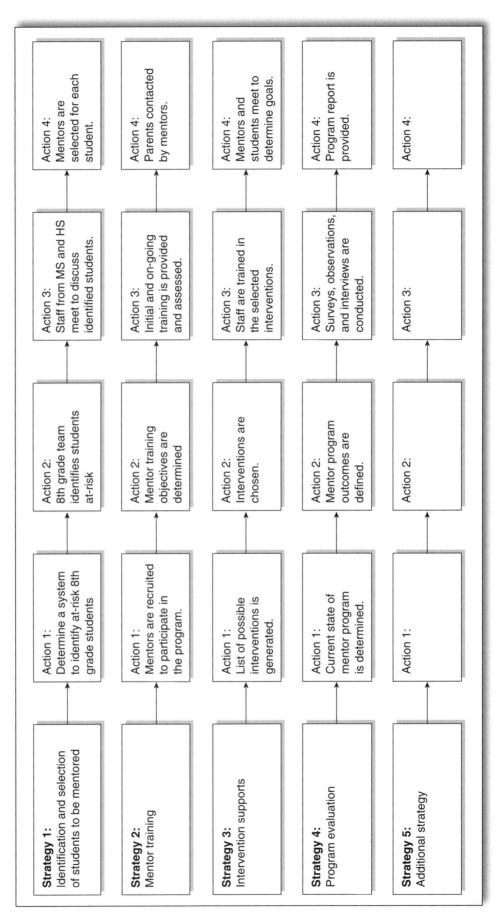

Figure 10.3   A New Model of Systemic Improvement

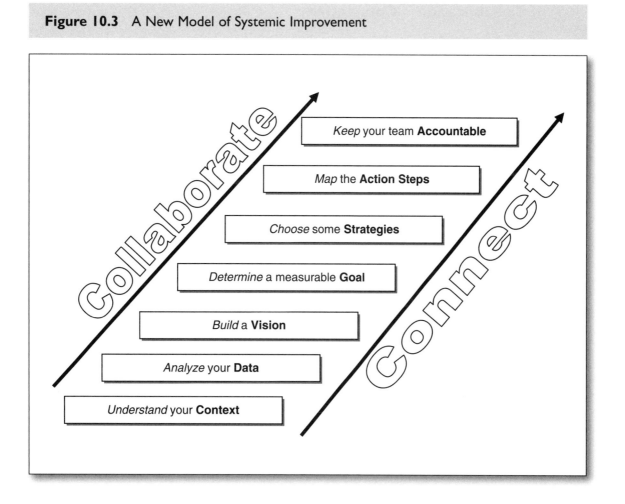

Running in Circles

The continuous improvement process has been well documented and described over the past 80 years. Beginning with Shewart's (1939) Plan, Do, Check, Act (PDCA) model as depicted in Figure 10.4 that was designed to improve factory production, manufacturing, and the precision of quality parts, we have learned through successive generations the importance of planning an improvement, implementing that improvement on a small scale, checking the impact of the action, and then acting upon what we have learned.

SIM is different than other improvement models. SIM is not designed so one can make better and better widgets. SIM focuses on learning and helping school teams learn together because learning is the work (Fullan, 2008).

Figure 10.4   Plan, Do, Check, Act

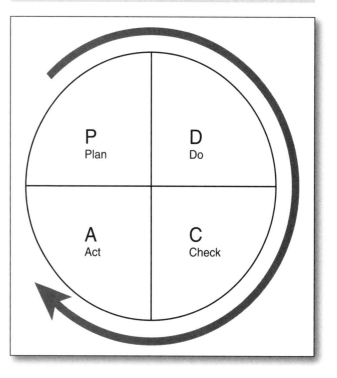

Collaboration = Connectivity

Education in the 21st century must be relevant and connect to student needs and interest. Our world is shrinking at an extremely rapid pace. Consider the phenomenon of Facebook. It all started in sophomore Mark Zuckerberg's dorm room at Harvard in 2004. There are now over 750 million Facebook users around the world, and the growth curve of people signing up shows no signs of flattening. The 25-year-old Zuckerberg could have cashed in his countless pile of chips a long time ago for an astronomical payday, but he hasn't. Why? Because he has a mission—that the world will be a more transparent and connected place, and he isn't willing to compromise on doing work that matters. The mission of Facebook is imprinted on the inside of the infamous "hoody" that Mark wears everywhere. It reads, "Facebook gives people the power to share and make the world more open and connected" (Tsotsis, 2010). But what does connectivity have to do with school improvement?

School improvement—now more so than ever—does not happen in a vacuum. Staff members must work together. They must collaborate around issues and tasks they value and have time built into their day to connect with each other regarding their practices, the data they are gathering and digesting, and the ways they will use that data. They must collaborate around standards, interventions, and student work. Psychologist Keith Sawyer (2007) in his book *Group Genius,* writes that all great inventions and innovations emerge from a sequence of small sparks and that collaboration actually is the vehicle for bringing the sparks together to achieve breakthrough results. Meaningful, sustained improvement does not happen without effective, ongoing collaboration. Connectivity is key, and in today's always-on world, there are infinite ways to connect.

Stepping Up to Collaboration

School improvement requires creative teams to move through the seven steps illustrated in figure 10.3:

1. Understand the context.

2. Analyze data.

3. Build a vision.

4. Determine a measurable goal.

5. Choose some strategies.

6. Map the action steps.

7. Keep your team accountable.

Improvement efforts must consider context. Before a team rushes into trying to make something better, it is essential to understand the context. If this step is omitted, one may end up with unintended consequences and problems bigger than the original ones. Context is background information. Context is the demographic data about the school, district, or classroom. We are all the products of our history. It is important to know who your students are, what their families are like, and the context of their surroundings.

Does the community have a high percentage of college graduates or a low percentage? What are the poverty percentages when one considers ethnicity and languages spoken? Even more importantly, what district or school initiatives have been tried in the past? What kind of teaching experiences and background do teachers possess? What kind of professional development have they participated in? What is important to them? What beliefs do they have and hold dear? Questions like these need to be asked and reflected upon when analyzing the context in which improvement will take place. The data generated from these questions need to be analyzed and synthesized. This process yields valuable information about how improvement might best be designed.

Context Is Critical

To illustrate the importance of context, a consultant was called to upstate New York to begin a peer-coaching program in a district. The purpose of implementing this program was to maximize resources teachers had available to them to address a diversity of students' learning needs. However, in asking questions about the context, the consultant learned that in this district there was a peer-assistance program for teachers with substandard evaluations. Obviously, the names of the two programs were too close for constituent comfort so the name was changed from peer coaching to collegial conversations before introducing the program to staff members. Michael Fullan once said in an informal conversation, "The proof is in the putting. How something is put forth will influence its success or failure."

Analyze Your Data

Analyzing data is the first thing to do once the context has been assessed. Analyzing data is the process of listening to and looking at your information. It may also include exploring information you don't have but need. Data analysis is not all about numbers. It is about relationships—what those numbers and observations mean. Drawing meaning and interpretation from data analysis is the most important aspect of this process and happens best when teams work together to analyze the data by asking questions. When taking on this important step, it is crucial to know and understand not just what the numbers are, but how to look at them and use them to guide instruction. Data—whether they are numbers gathered from assessments or notes gathered from observations and conversations—must be looked at in team settings in order to maximize its meaning.

Building a Vision

Building a vision occurs after the context has been explored and data have been examined and analyzed. Vision building is essential to implementation. Author Seth Godin refers to this as the process of "shipping." Being able to "ship"—to deliver a product, service, or in this case an effective improvement strategy—requires a vision or destination. Godin coined the term from an episode in the early days of Apple computer when founder Steve Jobs made the comment to programmers who were frantically perfecting code for the first Macintosh computer. Jobs said, "Real artists ship," and the point was clear (Godin, 2010a). Great, elegant ideas are worthless if a product isn't delivered. Being able to get something out the door is essential.

Educators can be enamored with the process of improvement—attending sessions, reading books, looking through all the data, and using all the acronyms without really making anything better. Without context-based action, little changes, even if the activity engages stakeholders in new programs. School improvement work must be based on the unique characteristics of the context and must be focused on achieving a shared vision or destination. When improvement efforts have been strategically aligned in this regard, progress is achieved.

Determining a Goal

Determining a goal and making it measurable is absolutely essential to helping teams get to the next level of improvement. However, goal setting should never be confused with priorities. Priorities are long-term commitments. Priorities do not change over time. They are the big ideas. Goal setting is different. Setting measurable and meaningful goals supports team members in their work to translate vision into action. Goals push the organization beyond the status quo toward a destination of enhanced achievement. Goals must be meaningful and measurable as well as stretch employees and inspire team members to engage and work to their full potential.

Choosing Strategies

Choosing strategies is the process of writing down the projects the team will take on that will impact achieving the goal. Strategies are actions to get organizational members moving toward accomplishing the goal. For instance, if the goal is to improve the percentage of students proficient in writing from 50% to 75% districtwide, the strategies to achieve that goal would include a number of projects, including, but not limited to additional professional development opportunities, increased writing opportunities across the curriculum—especially nonfiction writing, peer observation of demonstration lessons, the use of schoolwide writing prompts, collaborative scoring of writing samples emphasizing interrater reliability, and so on. Each of these strategies has additional action steps. Figures 10.1 (page 101) and 10.2 (page 108) illustrate how SIM can be used to visually delineate strategies to be implemented in order to attain a measurable goal.

Action Steps

Action steps break down each strategy into achievable activities that can be monitored. Almost like a to-do list, action steps map out the actions to be taken for an improvement to occur. Sketching out the action steps and then completing those steps is the best way to move teams toward achieving their goals. Action steps are the bottom line, essential to making progress. They must be clear and extremely easy to follow and understand. They tell you what to do next.

Accountability

Accountability is the final step of school improvement. Accountability is a crucial component to results and impacts everyone's performance in a positive way. Teams and team members who hold each other accountable in an encouraging way to motivate the team do great work. High-functioning teams serious about improvement constantly revisit and commit to their vision, declare their measurable goals, work together on strategies, and relentlessly pursue action steps. Accountability requires teams to do what they say they will do. Accountability ensures that team members will not quit when the going gets tough. Accountability requires exceptional leaders at all levels of the organization who are willing to have difficult conversations, examine their own actions critically, and support people through good times and discouraging times.

IN THE FIELD: HIGH SCHOOL MENTORING PROJECT

SIMs can chart improvement efforts and demonstrate results over time. In the fall of 2010, a comprehensive high school decided to take mentoring to the next level of achievement and used a SIM to sketch out its intentions (see Figure 10.2 on page 108). Led by an English Language Leaner (ELL) teacher leader, team members identified the following strategies: identification, training, and intervention to achieve the goal of reducing the number of students at risk of dropping out by creating meaningful connections with adults at school. As team members, they understood their own high school context and the research that states multiple mentors is the number-one way that students from backgrounds of poverty break the college barrier (Beagle, 2007). They inferred that all students—poverty impacted, ELL, special education identified, or emotionally at risk—could benefit from this intervention.

The action steps they planned in the area of identification included determining which eighth-grade students were at risk and could benefit from mentoring. Subsequent meetings were planned between teachers, administrators, and counselors to determine which students needed the extra support that mentoring could provide.

Under the strategy of training, they determined action steps that included professional development sessions twice a month with the mentors, contacting parents to generate their support, and meeting with students to explain the value of mentoring and the increased success they could expect in school as a result of being involved in the program. The strategy of intervention included specific action steps to support students in the school:

- Daily check-in, check-out accountability
- Teaching organizational skills including how to use a planner
- Setting academic and behavior goals

(Continued)

(Continued)

- Check-in with homework assignments
- Connecting the students to the academic center
- Teaching students how to be self-advocates
- Identifying a positive adult role model to talk with about issues occurring at school or at home
- Teaching strategies for learning how to navigate the academic system so they can get support and help from the right person at the right time
- Teaching lessons about communication with adults and finding help from staff in the building.
- Teaching strategies for learning with whom to make friends and how to keep them, plus how to deal with social situations and be involved with school
- Teaching strategies for completing homework at home
- Teaching time management and how to be productive outside of school including the importance of setting up a consistent schedule
- Providing a summer school kick start that connects students to adult and peer mentors

The time it took the improvement team to think through the map and put its strategies and actions on paper paid valuable dividends in terms of being able to implement this program successfully and accomplish the desired results—making a difference in the lives of students in a way that affected their life paths.

■ PUTTING IT ALL TOGETHER

In the *Six Secrets of Change* Michael Fullan (2008) writes about the "black box" of implementation. We know what to do—it is the doing of it—the changing of behavior that is the most difficult aspect of reform. SIMs help data teams embrace, engage, and work through the mystery of the black box and come out on the other end better, stronger, and more successful with demonstrated results. Much like how basketball great John Wooden sketched out his practices to get the most out of every minute, leadership teams that map out strategies and actions based upon their goals can work through the black box of implementation and will see measurable improvements occur on a regular basis. Outcomes improve by focusing on the specific processes that impact them, not by focusing on the outcomes. A coach like John Wooden comes along once a century, but we don't have to be a John Wooden to adopt his passion for improvement through process. We encourage you to experiment with using SIMs to support classroom, school, and district improvement. We wish you an enlightened and productive journey.

11

Now What?

Using the Tools in the Classroom, School, and District

We cannot do everything at once, but we can do something at once.

—Calvin Coolidge

We must approach professional learning communities (PLCs) and using data effectively with the urgency of Calvin Coolidge. We must *"do something at once"* if we are going to make a difference. Our final chapter is a collection of black-line masters of each tool along with suggestions for ways you can use the tool as an individual teacher, member of a team, or at the school or district level. As you explore these tools in your school improvement efforts, you can visit *www.thedatacoach.net* to post a message about how your experience with the tools supports your school improvement efforts and see how others have done the same.

TOOL 1: THE SMALLEY ◼ TEAM-BUILDING PERSONALITY TEST

(See page 123.)

This tool is a great way for team members to learn about each other's strengths and weaknesses in a nonthreatening way. Using the metaphor of four different animals, the tool matches personality traits to the characteristics of a lion, otter, golden retriever, and beaver. For a detailed description of the tool and how it is used, please see Chapter 1.

Classroom: The tool is used with students to help them understand and appreciate classmates along with putting together cooperative learning teams.

PLC & Data Teams: Use this activity at the beginning of each year as new teams are formed to help participants get to know each other. Assign roles to teammates based upon the strengths and weaknesses identified through this activity.

School/District Level: This tool is used to support any district-level support team that meets on a regular basis. Completing this activity helps team members to understand and appreciate each other to greater degrees. Understanding is the first step to building positive relationships.

■ TOOL 2: IDENTIFY THE PROBLEM

(See page 124.)

This tool is best used when team members are facing a complex problem that may require an adaptive solution. Instead of being frustrated by not knowing where to start, taking a team through this reflective activity can help them to get their thoughts and feelings on paper to move beyond shame, blame, and excuses.

Classroom: This tool is used by students to explore any problem they encounter in a science experiment or complex math problem. It can also be used in cooperative learning situations for teams of students who are working on a group presentation or project, or when an individual student or group of students are experiencing an interpersonal problem or conflict and they need to think through how to solve it.

PLC & Data Teams: When team members are facing inexplicable and discouraging test score results, poor attendance problems, or mobility rates, taking them through this template helps them to get past feelings of frustration and angst about the data and begin the conversation about what actions (e.g., using other tools) can be taken or tried next to see a better result or deal with the situation they are facing. The best way to help teams move past debilitating data is to help them make a commitment to take some kind of action and stay in the realm of controlling what they can control.

School/District Level: This tool is best used as a starting place for problems that have no clear solution. Whether that is trying to find efficiencies in an ever shrinking budget or having to deal with a difficult parent, a good first step is to identify the problem and get your bearings for a starting place.

■ TOOL 3: THREE GUIDING QUESTIONS

(See page 125.)

Systemic school and district improvement starts with teams of teachers and educators determining the knowledge and skills that each student needs to know and demonstrate during each grade level or unit of study. Often referred to as power standards or learning targets, data coming from formative and summative sources are not very useful if they do not measure something that is common and comparable. Schools and districts that have not locally developed their power standards or learning targets end up relying too heavily on outside assessments for their data and as a result are not able to use the data in very meaningful ways to adjust instruction.

Classroom: This tool is used individually by teachers to think through what they want each student to learn during a particular course of study. Taking the time to think through this first enables them to plan curriculum accordingly, check for understanding during instruction, and design assessments to help know when students have learned the knowledge or can demonstrate the skill. In proficiency-based settings students use this tool to plan how to demonstrate mastery toward clearly defined learning targets.

PLC & Data Teams: Determining clearly defined standards by teams of teachers and deciding how to measure progress toward those targets is the work. All of our talk about using data in meaningful ways hinges on people knowing, understanding, and believing in common standards. Having teams use this tool for one content area (reading, math, science) and one grade level (or defined period of time) is the best place to start.

School/District Level: It is up to the school and district to develop systems to communicate what the horizontal and vertical teams come up with throughout the process. Great work in PLCs or data teams can be quickly undone by poor school and district communication of what was decided or a lack of follow through from school leaders. Leaders need to recognize, share, and honor what teams come up with on a regular basis horizontally across grade levels and vertically across grade levels and schools.

TOOL 4: ANALYZE YOUR STUDENTS ■

(See page 126.)

Once clear targets have been established, we can go to the work of analyzing students according to those targets. This is where tool number 4 can be used effectively. Since we are only looking at one set of data, the most important element of this tool is to define the level of achievement necessary to determine whether extension or intervention is needed along with what level of intensity is required.

Classroom: Individual teachers use this tool to analyze any set of student data to a standard. We have seen teachers effectively use this tool at the elementary level to determine reading groups according to the fluency and comprehension curriculum-based assessments they administer. Teachers at the secondary level have used this tool with student grades to determine which students need additional support and resources in order to achieve success.

PLC & Data Team: Teachers at the elementary level have used this tool in grade-level groups to determine what kind of interventions students need as they plan how to deliver additional doses of instruction in reading and math. Many curriculums on the market today come with some sort of assessment system. Using those assessments in teacher teams and analyzing the student results with the triangle framework of this tool provides keen insight into how instruction needs to be modified or adjusted in order to maximize student learning and achievement outcomes.

School/District Level: Nearly every Response to Intervention (RTI) initiative uses this tool in some form to determine which students are the most in need of intervention and support. RTI is implemented at the school level but designed and coordinated at the district level. It is important when using this tool at the district level to make sure assessments, intervention strategies, and decision rules are consistent across schools. Since determining special education eligibility is a district decision that occurs at the school level, it is essential that coordination and communication occur to ensure the process is consistently applied. Using this tool to analyze individual students per grade level is a great activity for principals to use since it helps them know where precious resources should be spent to help each student make progress toward the defined standard. The same concept can be applied to a district with many schools to determine which schools need additional support and resources to achieve excellence.

■ TOOL 5: FOUR QUADRANTS

(See page 127.)

The Four Quadrant tool allows educators to analyze two sets of numbers, look for patterns, and use those patterns to intervene and take specific actions that result in measurable improvements in the data. The key to using the Four Quadrants effectively is to determine the acceptable achievement level for the data that have been collected so that students can be individually placed on the quadrants according to their need.

Classroom: A teacher can take any two sets of numbers for students and place them in a quadrant in order to understand whether their actions are achieving the intended result. For instance, we have seen a teacher exploring proficiency-based instruction using the Four Quadrants to measure the impact of homework on test scores. She wondered if the students who completed homework performed better on the tests. Using the Four Quadrants, she discovered that homework completion was directly correlated to higher test scores. The Four Quadrants is also a great tool for student use in a variety of science and math applications.

PLCs & Data Teams: Teacher teams can look at fluency and comprehension scores for groups of students to determine what intervention is required. Attendance and grade point average (GPA), attendance and grades, or grades and test scores are all variations that can be analyzed to discover patterns that make a difference once you have determined what key outcome you are trying to achieve.

School/District Level: A group of seniors in a high school statistics class wanted to see the relationship between freshman success, attendance, and eighth-grade test scores in reading. They defined freshman success as maintaining a GPA of 2.0 or higher because a 2.0 GPA closely correlated to students that did not receive any F's in their courses. High school graduation is based upon successful completion of credits, which can only be earned by passing classes. By using several four quadrant charts, they discovered that ninth-grade attendance was more predictive of high school success than meeting the eighth-grade reading standard. Their study is an example of how the Four Quadrants can be used at the district level to inform schools about the importance of emphasizing attendance as a success strategy.

TOOL 6: WAGON WHEEL ■

(See page 128.)

When it comes to analyzing three or more sets of numbers, the Wagon Wheel is the best tool to discover patterns and make decisions based upon those patterns. It is not as important to determine an achievement target when using the Wagon Wheel. The most important element is being clear on how you label each spoke of the wheel so that the data are easily charted, understood, and acted upon.

Classroom: Teachers can use the Wagon Wheel to chart the progress of a group of students toward a particular standard, whether that is a timed multiplication assessment or the number of errors on a spelling test. The tool can be used by students for charting assignments, activities, or projects that have single variables with multiple inputs or multiple variables exploring a single topic.

PLCs & Data Teams: A grade-level team at a large elementary school used a Wagon Wheel to display how each of the classes in the school did on local reading, math, and writing assessments. They were looking for patterns to see if one particular class consistently outperformed or underperformed other classes for the purpose of providing support and resources to those teachers. It was discovered through this process that one class did outperform the others, but it was also determined through the Wagon Wheel that the highest achieving class also had the fewest students on Individualized Education Programs (IEPs). From this data analysis, the team could not determine if instruction or the initial placement of students was the biggest factor in the test score results. Using the Wagon Wheel helps explore these challenging dilemmas.

School/District Level: Large districts can use a Wagon Wheel to chart the key factors they want to track at each of their schools: attendance, free and reduced lunch, mobility, teacher experience, percent of master's degrees, and so on to see if any of these factors make a difference in student achievement outcomes. A school can even use a Wagon Wheel to chart the amount of trash that is picked up in different areas of the school in order to determine the best location to place new garbage cans. Like most of these tools, imagination is the only limit to how the Wagon Wheel can be used in school improvement efforts.

■ TOOL 7: FIVE WHYS

(See page 129.)

As the first of the qualitative tools, the Five Whys tool helps educators to explore the potential reasons behind a perplexing problem. Always looking for something to do that can make a difference, the Five Whys tool forces us to pause, reflect, and take stock of our options, and choose actions that have the largest possible impact.

Classroom: The classroom uses for this tool are extensive. We have seen teachers use this tool to explore the causes of major wars and significant events in our history in addition to uses surrounding the exploration of a science experiment. Training students to ask *why* questions may be the single best thing we do to promote critical thinking. No one should ever grow out of asking *why* questions.

PLC & Data Teams: The Five Whys is a great tool in the setting of an IEP meeting to discuss why a student is not making the progress that is expected. It can also be used to help a team decide what actions are in their control and what actions are not in their control so they can focus their energy and efforts on actions that have the greatest impact.

School/District Level: Whether a school is trying to determine the reasons behind a low attendance rate or a district is exploring why persistent achievement gaps still exist, a Five Whys activity is a simple yet powerful way to help get everyone involved and working together to solve complex problems.

■ TOOL 8: RELATIONS DIAGRAM

(See page 130.)

Asking why is only the beginning of exploring complex problems. Another helpful technique is investigating what relationship each reason may or may not have to each other. Determining which cause drives other causes is crucial to making strategic improvements in your data. The effectiveness in using the Relations Diagram relies on having a group of people invested in solving the problem, participating together, and being able to identify the problem to be solved before rushing in with solutions.

Classroom: We have seen this tool used in the classroom by a teacher exploring the different reasons why students were not completing their schoolwork. Assumptions by the teacher turned out to be different than what was reflected in the student responses, and as a result, the students took ownership of the proposed solutions and the result was a significant increase in the percent of work completed in the class.

PLC & Data Teams: A team of educators used a Relations Diagram to determine why a particular student was not progressing on his IEP goals. It didn't take long for the team to change its strategy once the driving forces behind the lack of progress were determined. Whether a team is exploring the progress of one particular student, a group of students, class, or grade level a Relations Diagram is a great tool for tenacious PLCs focused on results.

School/District Level: A district leadership team used a Relations Diagram to determine why district transportation costs were so high and how to take strategic actions to reduce costs and add efficiencies to the operation. Any operation (including student learning) can be improved, and the Relations Diagram is a great way to do it.

TOOL 9: THE FISHBONE ■

(See page 131.)

Popularized by the founder of the modern continuous improvement model Edward Deming (1986), organizations have been using the Fishbone as a data tool for years. There are many variations of the tool, but the one presented in this book can be used to explore excellent data (so that it can be replicated and scale to other classrooms) or troubling data that need to be improved. Though the Fishbone can start with individual reflection, the most successful uses involve a team of people all providing input.

Classroom: Teams of students enjoy using a Fishbone to explore the reasons behind an event. Even the youngest of children can understand writing causes on the bones of the fish and discussing the importance of each cause. Individual teachers can use this tool as a concept organizer or prewriting tool to help students think critically about what they write before they begin writing. It is an excellent way to prime the pump so to speak and get those creative juices flowing before starting on a large assignment or project.

PLCs & Data Teams: Whether a team is looking at an outstanding result in a particular classroom or exploring why an entire grade level did poorly on the state assessment, the Fishbone focuses thinking, helps teammates move into action mode, and places the team on offense when dealing with their data.

School/District Level: When there are big fish to fry, the Fishbone can do the job by providing a framework for discussion. It is easy to feel overwhelmed by poor results or overconfident by good ones. Using a Fishbone eliminates both extremes by focusing the team on what worked and how to scale it or what failed and how to fix it.

TOOL 10: SCHOOL IMPROVEMENT MAPPING ■

(See page 132.)

The end of all data tracking and analysis should be action. Without the will to learn from and *to do something differently* there really isn't any value in all of the time and energy spent in data collection (Gladwell, 2002). The School Improvement Map (SIM) assures that action takes place. Determining the specific, measurable goal is the most important element of SIM. Once that goal is determined, completing a SIM is simply a matter of choosing several strategies and actions to go with each strategy. School and district improvement is not a linear process. Many times staff members do not know exactly what to do or how to do it, but they know where they want to go. A SIM helps chart the destination and sketch out multiple options for getting there so that arrival is more likely to occur.

Classroom: A SIM can be used by an individual teacher to help him or her think through what strategies and actions to take to achieve the determined end result. Any time a teacher or class wants to set a group goal, a SIM can help them get there.

PLC & Data Teams: When teams of teachers work on a specific, measurable goal together, the likelihood of achievement multiplies. Whether the goal is helping every student meet the standard or increasing attendance, the power of collaboration toward a common goal by writing it down increases the team's chance of achieving the goal.

School/District Level: Leadership teams, site councils, and management cabinets of any type benefit from completing SIMs and holding each other accountable for the results. Once a SIMs is assigned and completed, it is important that systemic feedback loops are created to keep teams accountable toward making progress toward the goal.

TOOL I

The Smalley Team-Building Personality Test

In the spaces provided identify the degree in which the following characteristics or behaviors most accurately describe you in work settings. You can evaluate each column individually or use each of the four numbers across each row for a different look at the same data. When you are done, add up the total for each column and see what the results mean in Figure 1.2 on page 9.

0 = not at all   1 = somewhat   2 = mostly   3 = very much

Column 1	Column 2	Column 3	Column 4
___Likes control	___Enthusiastic	___Sensitive	___Consistent
___Confident	___Visionary	___Calm	___Reserved
___Firm	___Energetic	___Nondemanding	___Practical
___Likes challenge	___Promoter	___Enjoys routine	___Factual
___Problem solver	___Mixes easily	___Relational	___Perfectionist
___Bold	___Fun-loving	___Adaptable	___Detailed
___Goal driven	___Spontaneous	___Thoughtful	___Inquisitive
___Strong willed	___Likes new ideas	___Patient	___Persistent
___Self-reliant	___Optimistic	___Good listener	___Sensitive
___Persistent	___Takes risks	___Loyal	___Accurate
___Takes charge	___Motivator	___Even-keeled	___Controlled
___Determined	___Very verbal	___Gives in	___Predictable
___Enterprising	___Friendly	___Indecisive	___Orderly
___Competitive	___Popular	___Dislikes change	___Conscientious
___Productive	___Enjoys variety	___Dry humor	___Discerning
___Purposeful	___Group oriented	___Sympathetic	___Analytical
___Adventurous	___Initiator	___Nurturing	___Precise
___Independent	___Inspirational	___Tolerant	___Scheduled
___Action oriented	___Likes change	___Peace maker	___Deliberate
___**Total Score**	___**Total Score**	___**Total Score**	___**Total Score**

1. For more information about this assessment, visit www.smalley.cc

Source: Smalley and Trent, 1999. Available at http://smalley.cc/marriage-assessments/free-personality-test

TOOL 2
Identify the Problem

1. What problem are you facing?
2. How do you feel about it?
3. What data do you have about your problem?
4. What is your data telling you?
5. What will you do about it?

TOOL 3
Three Guiding Questions

1. What critical knowledge and/or skills (learning targets) does each student need to know or be able to do during this unit/course of study?

2. How will we know when each student has learned it?

3. How will we respond when a student needs intervention or extension along the way so that each one can reach (or exceed) the learning target?

Source: DuFour, 2004

TOOL 4
Analyze Your Students

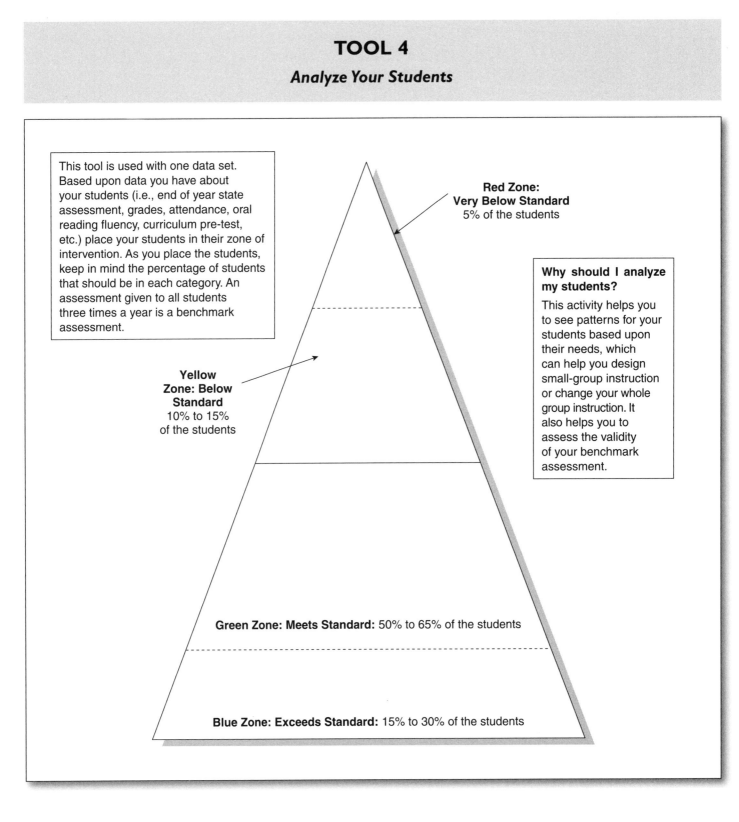

This tool is used with one data set. Based upon data you have about your students (i.e., end of year state assessment, grades, attendance, oral reading fluency, curriculum pre-test, etc.) place your students in their zone of intervention. As you place the students, keep in mind the percentage of students that should be in each category. An assessment given to all students three times a year is a benchmark assessment.

Red Zone: Very Below Standard
5% of the students

Why should I analyze my students?
This activity helps you to see patterns for your students based upon their needs, which can help you design small-group instruction or change your whole group instruction. It also helps you to assess the validity of your benchmark assessment.

Yellow Zone: Below Standard
10% to 15% of the students

Green Zone: Meets Standard: 50% to 65% of the students

Blue Zone: Exceeds Standard: 15% to 30% of the students

TOOL 5
Four Quadrants

Take two sets of data and plot the relationship between the data according to the corresponding quadrants. The visual representation will help you to analyze and identify patterns in the data and show you how to intervene effectively.

High

Quadrant I: Below the baseline in B. Above the baseline in A.	Quadrant II: Above the baseline in B. Above the baseline in A.
Quadrant III: Below the baseline in B. Below the baseline in A.	Quadrant IV: Above the baseline in B. Below the baseline in A.

Data Set A: _____

Low

Low   **Date Set B:** _____   **High**

TOOL 6
Wagon Wheel

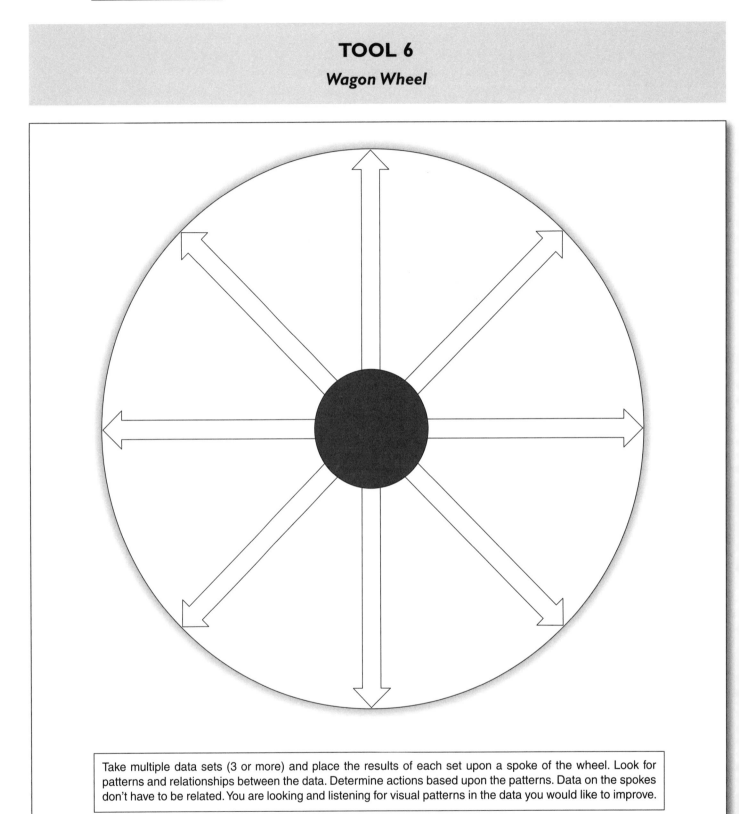

Take multiple data sets (3 or more) and place the results of each set upon a spoke of the wheel. Look for patterns and relationships between the data. Determine actions based upon the patterns. Data on the spokes don't have to be related. You are looking and listening for visual patterns in the data you would like to improve.

TOOL 7
Five Whys

Persistent Problem: _____

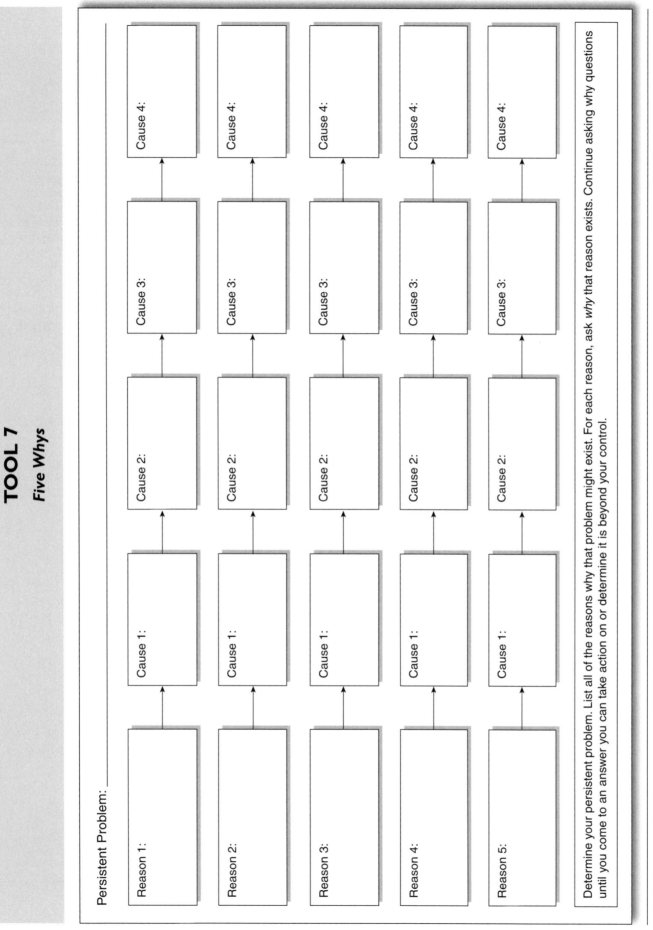

Reason 1:	→	Cause 1:	→	Cause 2:	→	Cause 3:	→	Cause 4:
Reason 2:	→	Cause 1:	→	Cause 2:	→	Cause 3:	→	Cause 4:
Reason 3:	→	Cause 1:	→	Cause 2:	→	Cause 3:	→	Cause 4:
Reason 4:	→	Cause 1:	→	Cause 2:	→	Cause 3:	→	Cause 4:
Reason 5:	→	Cause 1:	→	Cause 2:	→	Cause 3:	→	Cause 4:

Determine your persistent problem. List all of the reasons why that problem might exist. For each reason, ask *why* that reason exists. Continue asking why questions until you come to an answer you can take action on or determine it is beyond your control.

TOOL 8
Relations Diagram

A Relations Diagram is used for persistent, complex problems that have no apparent solutions. Data teams explore a problem by first thinking of all the possible causes and then using a "key driver" process to determine which causes are driving (or influencing) most of the other problems. The key driver process reveals which cause to address first with a proposed solution. Relation Diagrams help teams rally around targeted strategies and to develop the buy-in necessary to tackle persistent problems. The Relations Diagram process also helps teams avoid unintended consequences that can come with complex problems.

Cause 1:

Cause 8:

Cause 2:

Cause 7:

Problem Statement:

Cause 3:

Cause 6:

Cause 4:

Cause 5:

TOOL 9
The Fishbone

The Fishbone diagram tool is used to determine the reasons behind an outstanding result or cause for concern. On the "bones" of the fish, the team lists all of the possible reasons for a positive result. Using a fishbone diagram and writing an importance value beside each potential reason is helpful in determining which causes have the greatest impact upon the result.

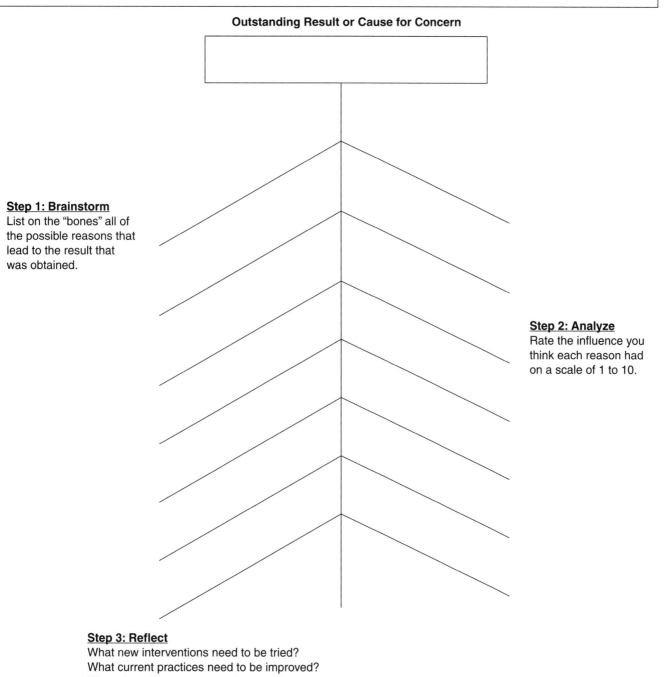

Outstanding Result or Cause for Concern

Step 1: Brainstorm
List on the "bones" all of the possible reasons that lead to the result that was obtained.

Step 2: Analyze
Rate the influence you think each reason had on a scale of 1 to 10.

Step 3: Reflect
What new interventions need to be tried?
What current practices need to be improved?
What should you stop doing?

TOOL 10

School Improvement Mapping

School improvement destination (goal): _____

Strategy 1:	→	Action 1:	→	Action 2:	→	Action 3:	→	Action 4:
Strategy 2:	→	Action 1:	→	Action 2:	→	Action 3:	→	Action 4:
Strategy 3:	→	Action 1:	→	Action 2:	→	Action 3:	→	Action 4:
Strategy 4:	→	Action 1:	→	Action 2:	→	Action 3:	→	Action 4:
Strategy 5:	→	Action 1:	→	Action 2:	→	Action 3:	→	Action 4:

References

Abell, J. (2009, August 9). Aug. 6, 1997: Apple rescued — by Microsoft. *Wired*. Retrieved from http://www.wired.com/thisdayintech/2009/08/dayintech_0806/

Barth, R. (2001). *Learning by heart*. San Francisco, CA: Jossey-Bass.

Beagle, D. (2007). *See poverty . . . Be the difference*. Portland, OR: Communication Across Barriers.

Block, P. (2003). *The answer to how is yes: Acting on what matters*. San Francisco, CA: Berrett-Koehler.

Carmichael, E. (n.d.). Lesson #4: Create a high hiring bar [Web log post]. Retrieved from http://www.evancarmichael.com/Famous-Entrepreneurs/959/Lesson-4-Create-a-High-Hiring-Bar.html

Carson, B. (2006). *Think big: Unleashing your potential for excellence*. Grand Rapids, MI: Zondervan.

Castillo, S. (2011, August 18). Adding a touch of class [Online forum]. Retrieved from http://www.ode.state.or.us/news/announcements/announcement.aspx?ID=7562&TypeID=4

Chenoweth, K. (2007). *"It's being done": Academic success in unexpected schools*. Cambridge, MA: Harvard Education Press.

Childress, S., Doyle, D., & Thomas, D. (2009). *Leading for equity: The pursuit of excellence in the Montgomery County public schools*. Cambridge, MA: Harvard Education Press.

City, E., Elmore, R., Fiarman, S., & Teitel, L. (2009). *Instructional rounds in education: A network approach to improving teaching and learning*. Cambridge, MA: Harvard Education Press.

Collins, J. (2001). *Good to great*. New York, NY: Harper Business.

The College Board. (n.d.). Our president [Web post]. Retrieved from http://about.collegeboard.org/leadership/president

Conley, D. (2010). *College and career ready: Helping all students succeed beyond high school*. San Francisco, CA: Jossey-Bass.

Covey, S. (2004). *The seven habits of highly effective people*. Salt Lake City, UT: Free Press.

Deming, E. (1986). *Out of the crisis*. Boston, MA: MIT Press.

DuFour, R. (2004). What is a "professional learning community?" *Educational Leadership*, *61*(8), 6–11.

Esquith, R. (2004). *There are no shortcuts*. New York, NY: Anchor.

Esquith, R. (2007). *Teach like your hair's on fire*. New York, NY: Viking Adult.

Fielding, L., Kerr, N., & Rosier, P. (2007). *Annual growth for all students: Catch-up growth for those who are behind*. Seattle, WA: New Foundation Press.

Freeman, C. (2010, July 13). Official: Chicks before eggs. *The Sun*. Retrieved from http://www.thesun.co.uk/sol/homepage/news/3052244/Official-Chicks-before-eggs.html

Fullan, M. (2008). *Six secrets of change*. San Francisco, CA: Jossey-Bass.

Fullan, M., Crévola, P., & Hill, C. (2006). *Breakthrough*. Thousand Oaks, CA: Corwin.

Gladwell, M. (2002, July 22). The myth of talent. *The New Yorker*, 28–33.

Gladwell, M. (2008, December 15). Most likely to succeed. *The New Yorker*. Retrieved from http://www.newyorker.com/reporting/2008/12/15/081215fa_fact_gladwell

Godin, S. (2010a). *Linchpin: Are you indispensable?* New York, NY: Portfolio Hardcover.

Godin, S. (2010b, October 11). You don't need a permit [Web log post]. Retrieved from www.sethgodin.com

Godin, S. (2010c, November 23). Reasons to work [Web log post]. Retrieved from www .sethgodin.com

The Governance Institute. (2006, May 1). 100,000 Lives Campaign Results. Retrieved http://www.governanceinstitute.com/ResearchPublications/ResourceLibrary/ tabid/185/CategoryID/7/List/1/Level/a/ProductID/662/Default.aspx?SortFiel d=ProductName%2CDateCreated

Heath, C., & Heath, D. (2010). *Switch: How to change when change is hard.* New York, NY: Crown Business.

Hess, R. (2005). *Excellence, equity, efficiency.* Lanham, MD: Roman & Littlefield.

Hess, R. (2011). *Administrative professional growth and accountability handbook.* Lebanon, OR: Lebanon Community Schools.

Horner, R., & Todd, A. (2010, February). *Team initiated problem solving.* Paper presented at the Coaches Conference at Oregon State University.

Houghton Mifflin Harcourt. (n.d.). *Harcourt Quick Mastery Theme test.* Retrieved from http://www.hmhschool.com/School/index.html

Lemov, D. (2010). *Teach like a champion: 49 techniques that put students on the path to college.* San Francisco, CA: Jossey-Bass.

Lencioni, P. (2002). *The five dysfunctions of a team.* San Francisco, CA: Jossey-Bass.

Lopez, D. (2009). *No excuses university: Hundreds of schools, thousands of students, one big dream.* San Diego, CA: Turnaround Schools.

Matthews, J. (2010). Great schools in unlikely places. *Newsweek.* Retrieved from http:// www.thedailybeast.com/newsweek/videos/2009/06/08/great-schools-in- unlikely-places-corbett-or.html

Miller, D. (2003). *Blue like jazz.* Nashville, TN: Thomas Nelson.

Miller, D. (2011). *Father fiction.* Brentwood, TN: Howard Books.

Moulton, M. W. (1999). *Emotions of normal people.* London, UK: Routledge.

NCHEMS Information Center. (n.d.). *Progress and completion: Graduation rates by state.* Retrieved December 15, 2010, from www.higheredinfo.org: http://www.highe redinfo.org/dbrowser/?year=2008&level=nation&mode=graph&state=0&submeas ure=27

Penelope & Corps. (1990). *School culture assessment tool.* Retrieved from www.breakthrough schools.org/culture

Pink, D. (2010). *Drive: The surprising truth about what motivates us.* New York, NY: Riverhead.

Ravitch, D. (2011, February). Will school reform really improve our schools? Paper presented at the AASA Conference. Denver, CO.

Reeves, D. (2006). *The learning leader.* Alexandria, VA: Association for Curriculum and Development.

Reeves, D. (2009). *Leading change in your school: How to conquer myths, build commitment, and get results.* Alexandria, VA: ASCD.

Reeves, D. (2010, May 19). Leadership and learning [Web log post]. Retrieved http:// www.leadandlearn.com/blog?page=3

Sawyer, K. (2007). *Group genius: The creative power of collaboration.* New York, NY: Basic Books.

Schlechty, P. (2002). *Working on the work: An action plan for teachers, principals, and super- intendents.* San Francisco, CA: Jossey-Bass.

Schmoker, M. (2011). *Focus: Elevating the essentials to radically improve student learning.* Alexandria, VA: ASCD.

Scott, S. (2004). *Fierce conversations: Achieving success at work and in life one conversation at a time.* New York, NY: Berkley Trade.

Shewart, W. (1939). *Statistical method from the viewpoint of quality control.* New York, NY: Dover.

Sisodia, R., Wolfe, D., & Sheth, J. (2007). *Firms of endearment.* Upper Saddle River, NJ: Wharton School.

Smalley, G., & Trent, J. (1999). *The two sides of love.* Carol Stream, IL: Tyndale House. Retrieved from http://smalley.cc/marriage-assessments/free-personality-test

Smart, B. (2005). *Topgrading: How leading companies win by hiring, coaching, and keeping the best people.* New York, NY: Portfolio Hardcover.

Smart, G., & Street, R. (2008). *Who: A method for hiring.* New York, NY: Ballantine Books.

Suess, D., Prelutsky, J., & Smith, L. (1998). *Hooray for Diffendoofer day!* New York, NY: Knopf Books for Young Readers.

Thims, L. (2008, December 16). *Philosophy: Which came first, the chicken or the egg?* Retrieved from http://www.helium.com/items/1267717-chicken-and-egg-paradox

Tsotsis, A. (2010, June 4). Zuckerberg's bizarre facebook insignia revealed, and what it means [Web log post]. Retrieved from http://blogs.sfweekly.com/thesnitch/2010/06/bizarre_facebook_insignia_reve.php

Wagner, T. (2010). *The global achievement gap.* New York, NY: Basic Books.

White, S. (2005). *Show me the proof.* Englewood, CO: Advanced Learning Press.

Whittaker, T. (2003). *What great teachers do differently: 14 things that matter most.* Larchmont, NY: Eye on Education.

Wooden, J., & Jamison, S. (2005). *Wooden on leadership: How to create a winning organization.* Columbus, OH: McGraw-Hill.

Wooden, J., & Yeager, D. (2009). *Game plan for life: The power of mentoring.* New York, NY: Bloomsbury.

Index

CORWIN
A SAGE Company

The Corwin logo—a raven striding across an open book—represents the union of courage and learning. Corwin is committed to improving education for all learners by publishing books and other professional development resources for those serving the field of PreK–12 education. By providing practical, hands-on materials, Corwin continues to carry out the promise of its motto: **"Helping Educators Do Their Work Better."**